STEVEN J. LAWSON

HEAVEN HELP US!

TRUTHS ABOUT ETERNITY THAT WILL HELP YOU LIVE TODAY

NAVPRESS

BRINGING TRUTH TO LIFE
NavPress Publishing Group
P.O. Box 35001, Colorado Springs, Colorado 80935

The Navigators is an international Christian organization. Jesus Christ gave His followers the Great Commission to go and make disciples (Matthew 28:19). The aim of The Navigators is to help fullfill that commission by multiplying laborers for Christ in every nation.

NavPress is the publishing ministry of The Navigators. NavPress publications are tools to help Christians grow. Although publications alone cannot make disciples or change lives, they can help believers learn biblical discipleship, and apply what they learn to their lives and ministries.

Library of Congress Catalog Card Number: 95-8616
ISBN 08910-99123

Cover photograph: Photodisk

Some of the anecdotal illustrations in this book are true to life and are included with the permission of the persons involved. All other illustrations are composites of real situations, and any resemblance to people living or dead is coincidental.

All Scripture quotations in this publication are taken from the *New American Standard Bible* (NASB), © The Lockman Foundation 1960, 1962, 1963, 1968, 1971, 1972, 1973, 1975, 1977.

Lawson, Steven J.
     Heaven help us! : truths about eternity that will help you live today / Steven J. Lawson.
        p.   cm.
     ISBN 0-89109-912-3
      1. Bible. N.T. Revelation IV–V—Commentaries.
    2. Bible. N.T. Revelation XXI-XXII–Commentaries.
    I. Title.
BS2825.3.L36   1995
228'.06–dc20   95-8616
                                          CIP

Printed in the United States of America

1 2 3 4 5 6 7 8 9 10 11 12 13 14 15 / 00 99 98 97 96 95

Contents

This book is dedicated to
my father and mother,
Dr. James W. and Betty Lawson,
who raised me in a Christian home,
who personally led me to faith in Christ,
and who have lovingly supported me
throughout my entire life

Hear, my son, your father's instruction,
And do not forsake your mother's teaching.
PROVERBS 1:8

Acknowledgments

———～———

By His grace, God has helped me greatly through the lives of several significant people in the writing of this book. Just as the Apostle Paul was surrounded by a circle of friends who supported him in his ministry, so I have been greatly supported by many others in this endeavor. I want to thank:

Steve Webb, editorial director at NavPress, who first believed in this project and who has offered much encouragement and editorial skills in refining this book.

Jeff Kinley, Todd Murray, Curtis Thomas, and James Henrich, my fellow pastors at The Bible Church of Little Rock, who have been a vast reservoir of theological insight, creative thinking, editorial suggestions, and personal support.

Bill Eubanks, close friend and pastor, graciously read the manuscript with me and helped in its revision, offering "theological fiber" to bolster the weightiness of the message.

Sherry Humphres, my personal secretary, who faithfully typed the manuscript under the stress of my many deadlines.

Dr. Adrian Rogers, my former pastor, whose ministry continues to shape my thinking and influence every word that I write.

Anne, my wife, and my four children—Andrew, James, Grace Anne, John—have fervently prayed for me that the writing of this book would be God-honoring and a particular blessing to your spiritual life. Any successful ministry that this book will have may be traced back to the prayers of my wife and children.

Chapter One

HEAVEN CAN'T WAIT!

The Priority of Heaven

Revelation 4:1

———⟋~⟍———

I WANT TO DESTROY A DEADLY *HERESY.*

Someone said it years ago, without thinking. And we've been believing it ever since. It's one of those catchy sayings repeated so many times that it's now canonized and accepted as inspired Scripture.

Say it and people will nod in agreement with you. Repeat it and others think you're a sage of sorts, a modern-day guru. It sounds so pithy, like something Solomon might have said in Proverbs.

You may even believe it yourself.

So what is this *lethal* lie, you ask?

What could possibly be so threatening to your Christian life? What is so potentially dangerous to your relationship with God? Well, hold on. Brace yourself. Here it is:

"He's so heavenly minded, he's no earthly good."

Sound familiar? Sure, you say, but what's so bad about *that?* How could that seemingly innocent little saying be so destructive?

Now, before you begin to argue with me, trust me—you won't find it anywhere in the Bible. There's no chapter and verse for it. No biblical citation. No cross-reference. In fact, just the opposite is taught in Scripture.

To the contrary, God calls us to be *so* heavenly minded that we *are* of earthly good. The truth is, a mind set on heavenly realities must govern all our earthly pursuits. The

10

Bible says, "Set your mind on the things above, not on the things that are on earth" (Colossians 3:2).

Let's be honest. Too many of us have this all backwards. We're so earthly minded that we're no heavenly good. If only we were *more* heavenly minded.

All too often we live shallow, earthbound lives that are preoccupied with the temporal. We're caught up in the trivial pursuit of the here and now. In the midst of our hectic schedules, we give *too little* thought to eternal things above—*not too much*. We must be more heavenly minded if we are to be any earthly good.

Is that *really* true? Do we need to be *more* heavenly minded if we are to be of earthly good?

Consider the Lord Jesus Christ. Was there ever anyone who walked this earth more heavenly minded than He? Of course not! No man ever lived in closer contact with Heaven than Christ. But wouldn't we also say that no one ever accomplished more earthly good than He did? Certainly! Fact is, Jesus was so heavenly minded that He *was* earthly good.

The same passion must drive and dominate our lives. If we are to be more like Christ, we must be more heavenly minded—or our lives will never have an impact on this world. We must live for things *unseen*, not things that are *seen*. We must live for *eternal* realities, not those that are *temporal*.

The Apostle Paul put it this way: "We look not at the things which are seen, but at the things which are not seen; for the things which are seen are temporal, but the things which are not seen are eternal" (2 Corinthians 4:18).

So why do we say it?

"He's so heavenly minded, he's no earthly good."

Because all too often it reflects our out-of-whack priorities. By adopting this worldly philosophy, we can still live our earthbound lives without having to change. It soothes our consciences. It pampers our lifestyles. It reflects the carnal condition of our hearts.

But you may say, "Yeah, I know people who read their Bibles, but their lives never amount to anything. See there, you can be so heavenly minded that you're no earthly good."

Let me tell you, such a person may sit in church regularly and even read his Bible daily. But that doesn't mean he's heavenly minded, any more than sitting in a garage makes him a car. A *true* heavenly mindset will effect change in our lives from the inside-out.

So, what *exactly* does it mean to be heavenly minded? What does it mean to set your mind on things above?

To be heavenly minded means to live a life of faith in things not seen (Hebrews 11:1). It means to live for the world to come, not this present world. It means to see all of life from an eternal perspective. It means to live every day and weigh every decision in the light of eternity. It means to live for that which is *timeless,* not temporal; to live for that which is *spiritual,* not tangible; to live for that which is *invisible,* not visible.

In short, the one who is heavenly minded has one overwhelming passion in life—*God!*

If we are to be heavenly minded, our entire disposition should be oriented toward the unseen realities of the kingdom of God. Only then can we rightly enjoy the things of this world. Jesus said, "Seek first His kingdom and His righteousness; and all these things shall be added to you" (Matthew 6:33).

We may think the burning issue of life presently is to get our marriage in order. Or get on the right career path. Or get our finances straightened out. But as important as these pressing issues are, our greatest need must be to become absorbed with the glory of God. Why? Because only those who are consumed with God will be internally changed and, as a result, see their marriage, work, and finances put right.

John Piper hit the nail on the head when he wrote, "The greatness and the glory of God are relevant. It does not matter if surveys turn up a list of perceived needs that does not include the supreme greatness of the sovereign God of grace. That is the deepest need. Our people are starving for God."[1]

12

How about you? Do you sense your hunger for God? Do you thirst for more of Heaven in your heart?

HUNGRY HEARTS, RESTLESS SOULS

Deep within every human heart there is a restless longing for eternity. Innately, our souls long for a place called Heaven. Heaven—not this world—is the real home of all who put their trust in Jesus Christ.

As people created in the image of God, every one of us possesses a God-consciousness. God has put eternity in our hearts, the Bible says—a yearning for Heaven. As the crown of God's creation, we have been made in His likeness and, thus, we long for eternity!

Wherever men live on the face of the earth—whether in the deepest heart of Africa, in the South Seas, or in the largest cosmopolitan cities of the world—they believe in an afterlife. Intuitively, they believe they will live forever. Instinctively they believe in a place called Heaven, whatever they may call it. We all long for a place called Heaven.

As believers in Jesus Christ, it is only natural for us to feel this way. Everything we value most awaits us in Heaven. God and Christ reside in Heaven. Family and loved ones await us there. Our true inheritance and heavenly citizenship are reserved for us in Heaven. Our eternal reward and spiritual treasure are laid up there. True happiness and perfect health can only be found there.

No wonder our hearts long for Heaven!

Deep within our inner man, the human spirit groans to rid itself of this mortal flesh and enter into the very presence of God to enjoy Him forever. That one holy passion—placed within us by God Himself—cries out from the depths of our being for eternity.

Unfortunately, despite this God-given longing for Heaven, we have become too attached to this world. Instead of laying up treasure in Heaven, we treasure the riches of this earth. Resisting the inner voice of conscience, we tell ourselves, "Heaven can wait."

But Heaven *can't* wait!

No way!

We must live for eternity *today*!

How can we recapture our passion for Heaven? How can we live for an unseen future world rather than for this one?

Answering these questions, and many more, will be the pursuit of this book. In an attempt to increase our intense longing for eternity, we want to discover what the Scriptures reveal about our eternal home in Heaven and the One who reigns in majesty there. *Heaven, help us!*

GUIDED TOUR OF HEAVEN

Without a doubt, the most vivid and dramatic portrayal of Heaven found anywhere in Scripture is contained in the book of Revelation. The word *Heaven* is found more frequently in Revelation than any other New Testament book. In the Apocalypse, we are privileged to be given a spectacular vision of Heaven—a vision of unseen glory like nowhere else in Scripture.

In the course of this book, we will look at four chapters of Revelation. Specifically, we will look at Revelation 4–5 and 21–22. These two sections serve as bookends that bracket the prophetic section of John's vision. These chapters rend the veil covering the unseen world of Heaven and give us a glimpse into eternity. Beginning in Revelation 4, the Apostle John is taken on a guided tour of Heaven and shown the glory of Jesus Christ and our eternal dwelling place in breathtaking fashion. What he records in the Revelation commands our attention, sharpens our eternal perspective, and will change our lives forever.

Here's the setting. At the end of the first century, the Apostle John is exiled on the island of Patmos in the Mediterranean, where he is persecuted for his faith in Jesus Christ. Unexpectedly, he is confronted by the risen Christ. The Sovereign Lord of the Church—Jesus Christ—dramatically interrupts John's personal worship experience and speaks to him with an authoritative voice like a trumpet. As the aged apostle turns to see who is speaking, he sees the glorified Lord walking in the midst of His Church. His hair is white, His eyes blazing, His feet glowing like bronze in a furnace, and out of His mouth comes the Word of God (Revelation 1:10-16).

Overwhelmed by the vision, John collapses like a dead man before the risen Christ. With tender mercy, Jesus reaches out and lays His nail-pierced hand upon His trembling servant, giving him a reassuring touch of comfort and strength. In this dramatic encounter, Christ commissioned John to write seven letters to seven churches in Asia Minor (Revelation 1:17-20). In obedience to this heavenly vision, John penned and dispatched seven personalized epistles to the churches (Revelation 2–3).

But Christ is not through with John—not yet!

One more part of the vision remains. John must be given a guided tour of Heaven and shown what will take place in the future (Revelation 4–22). It is the remaining part of this book—the prophetic vision—to which we direct ourselves in this book. Specifically, we will look at the glories of God and Jesus Christ in Heaven, as well as our future celestial home, recorded in Revelation 4–5 and 21–22. These chapters are the beginning and ending of the futuristic section of the Apocalypse.

So come with me for the journey of a lifetime. As you turn the pages of this book, we will accompany John on his incredible whirlwind tour of Heaven. We will experience what we are destined to one day enjoy—the unseen realm of eternity—with the hope that it will dramatically impact our lives today and forever!

Buckle your seat belt.

The tour of Heaven now begins.

KNOCKING ON HEAVEN'S DOOR
While on the island of Patmos, John looks upward into the sky and sees a never-to-be-forgotten sight—Heaven!

After these things I looked, and behold, a door standing open in heaven. (Revelation 4:1)

With apostolic astonishment, he sees a door that has swung open in Heaven. It leads down a long corridor into the very throne room of God. The door provides access into the immediate presence of God, where the Almighty sits enthroned in majestic sovereignty. Through this door, John will see his first glimpse of Heaven.

At the present, Heaven is a closed book to mortal man. Unseen realms of celestial glory lie shrouded behind a dark veil of mystery. We are unable to look into the invisible world of Heaven with our natural eyes. On the other side of this open door lies what our eyes cannot now see—the unseen world of eternity.

Incredibly, John will be privileged to enter into the inner chamber of Heaven where God Himself resides and reigns. He will be given a rare glimpse into glory. The apostle will be admitted into the true Holy of Holies to see the supreme Headquarters of all the universe.

Make no mistake about it, Heaven is a *real* place. It is not a state of mind. Not a figment of man's imagination. Not a philosophical concept. Not a religious abstraction. Not a sentimental dream. Not the medieval fancy of an ancient scientist. Not the worn-out superstition of a liberal theologian. It's an actual place. A location far more real than where you presently live.

Jesus Himself called Heaven a real place (Greek word, *topos*). "In My Father's house are many dwelling *places*; if it were not so, I would have told you; for I go to prepare a *place* for you. And if I go and prepare a *place* for you, I will come again, and receive you to Myself; that where I am, there you may be also" (John 14:2-3, emphasis added). Yes, Heaven is a real *place*. Jesus said so.

Heaven is populated by *real* people, entered by *real* gates, traveled by *real* streets, and developed with *real* buildings. It is a *real* place where God lives. It is the *real* place from which Christ came into this world. And it is the *real* place to which Christ returned at His ascension—*really!*

PROPHET SHARING

Actually, John was not the first prophet to gaze into Heaven and record what He saw. The prophet Ezekiel also saw Heaven open up, allowing him to look into the invisible

16

world above. Right before his awestruck eyes, Ezekiel saw the unveiled glory of God.

> *Now it came about in the thirtieth year, on the fifth day of the fourth month, while I was by the river Chebar among the exiles,* the heavens were opened *and I saw visions of God.* (Ezekiel 1:1)

The same supernatural phenomenon occurred when Jesus was baptized in the river Jordan. Heaven opened up and the Holy Spirit descended to earth while God spoke audibly. This signified open communication between Heaven and earth.

> *And after being baptized, Jesus went up immediately from the water, and behold,* the heavens were opened, *and he saw the Spirit of God descending as a dove, and coming upon Him.* (Matthew 3:16)

Stephen was one of the early church's stalwarts of the faith. He, too, saw Heaven opened up. While he was being martyred for his uncompromising message, a door in Heaven was opened and Stephen beheld the glory of God.

> *But being full of the Holy Spirit, he gazed intently into heaven and* saw the glory of God, *and Jesus standing at the right hand of God; and he said,* "Behold, I see the heavens opened up *and the Son of Man standing at the right hand of God."* (Acts 7:55-56)

Furthermore, the Apostle Peter was privileged to see Heaven opened up. A door was opened in Heaven and an object lesson descended from above while the voice of God spoke directly from Heaven to Peter.

> *He beheld* the sky opened up, *and a certain object like a great sheet coming down, lowered by four corners to the ground, and there were in it all kinds of four-footed animals and crawling creatures of the earth and birds of the*

17

*air. And a voice came to him, "Arise, Peter, kill, and eat!"
But Peter said, "By no means, Lord. . . ."* (Acts 10:11-14)

Finally, once more in the book of Revelation, the Apostle John will see this same door opened in Heaven—a door through which Christ will pass to return to earth at His Second Coming. In that day, Heaven will open up and Christ will descend to earth in great power and blazing glory to consume His enemies.

I saw heaven opened; *and behold, a white horse, and
He who sat upon it is called Faithful and True; and in
righteousness He judges and wages war.* (Revelation 19:11)

We can conclude that whenever a door opened in Heaven, it signified that God was revealing His glory to man on earth. It announced a "strange encounter" of a divine kind! God must take the divine initiative to reveal Heaven to man. The doorknob is on His side. And when God opens the door of Heaven, we must sit up and take notice.

HEAVEN'S WAKE-UP CALL

From beyond this mysterious door in Heaven comes a voice—a familiar voice. A loud voice that John has heard previously. It is an authoritative voice like a shrill trumpet blast—powerful, dominating, overpowering, compelling, militant, victorious!

*The first voice which I had heard, like the sound of a
trumpet speaking with me, said, "Come up here, and I
will show you what must take place after these things."*
(Revelation 4:1)

Earlier, the apostle was in the Spirit on the Lord's day and heard this very same voice like a trumpet speaking to him. In this first part of the vision, John discovered that this voice was none other than Jesus Christ Himself (Revelation 1:9-20). Now, a second time, Jesus calls out to John.

The apostle is summoned by Christ Himself, "Come up

18

here." He is invited to come up into Heaven and enter through this open door.

Where is Heaven located?

Up!

Heaven is a real place on God's map, and it's located *up!* The very name, Heaven, means "up." The Hebrew word translated "Heaven" *(shamayim)* means height and is in the plural, meaning great heights, or the highest height. By its very name, we can conclude that Heaven is the highest point in all God's creation—the apex of the universe.

Similarly, the Greek word for Heaven (ouranos), from which we get the name of the planet Uranus, means "an elevated place" or "a place that is highly lifted up." Heaven is raised up—elevated far above the planets, beyond the galaxies and the solar systems.

At His incarnation, Jesus came down to the earth, and when He left He ascended up to Heaven (Ephesians 4:8-10). When Jesus comes again, He will descend down from Heaven, at which time the Church will be caught up to Heaven (1 Thessalonians 4:16-17). Similarly, the new Jerusalem will come down from Heaven (Revelation 21:2).

When Satan attempted to exalt himself above God's throne, he boasted, "I will ascend to heaven, I will raise my throne above the stars of God, and I will sit on the mount of assembly in the recesses of the north. I will ascend above the heights of the clouds" (Isaiah 14:13-14). Heaven is located in the uppermost far recesses of the north, as high up as one can possibly go. Far above the stars. Far above the clouds.

Interestingly enough, the Bible teaches that there are three heavens. The Apostle Paul wrote that, much like John's experience, he was caught up into the "third heaven" (2 Corinthians 12:2). A third heaven implies, quite logically, that there must be a first and second heaven. A third heaven means that there are three stratas, or layers, of elevated places above the earth. So, what's the difference?

The first heaven refers to the lower atmosphere that immediately surrounds the planet earth. Scientists call it the troposphere. It is the lower strata where clouds form, birds fly, and airplanes travel. The Bible says, "The rain and the snow come down from heaven" (Isaiah 55:10). Also,

Sing praise to our God on the lyre,
Who covers the heavens with clouds,
Who provides rain for the earth." (Psalm 147:7-8)

The second heaven is higher than the first. It is the outer space where the stars, moons, and planets exist. Massive in proportion, this heaven contains the realms of planetary galaxies where the celestial bodies orbit. "Then God said, 'Let there be lights in the expanse of the new heavens to separate the day from the night, . . . and let them be for lights in the expanse of the heavens to give light on the earth. . . .' And God placed them in the expanse of the heavens to give light on the earth" (Genesis 1:14-17).

The third heaven is the place where God lives—the highest heaven of all. It is the divine dwelling place upon high. "The LORD looks from heaven; He sees all the sons of men; from His dwelling place He looks out on all the inhabitants of the earth" (Psalm 33:13-14). "For He looked down from His holy height; from heaven the LORD gazed upon the earth" (102:19). This highest tier of Heaven is far above the earth's lower atmosphere. Far beyond outer space. Far beyond the solar systems.

That's where Heaven is—up!

Thus, John is summoned to come up to the world of Heaven.

Why?

Because God wants to show John worldly events from a heavenly perspective. He invites John up to Heaven in order to see earthly affairs from an eternal perspective. Only from the heights of Heaven can John see as God sees.

The same is true for us. Only from an elevated, eternal perspective can we see life as God sees it. As we view world events and our personal circumstances, we must always interpret them through the grid of an eternal perspective.

THE JOURNEY OF A LIFETIME

In response to the divine voice, John now embarks upon the trip of a lifetime. He is instantaneously catapulted into Heaven.

> *Immediately, I was in the Spirit . . . in heaven.*
> (Revelation 4:2)

Dramatically, John was raptured in his spirit to Heaven. While the apostle's body remained on the isle of Patmos, his inner man was transported by the Holy Spirit above the natural order of time and space to enter the heavenly realm. This spiritual state was more than just a vision or dream. John is actually taken to Heaven to see what physical eyes cannot see and to hear what natural ears cannot hear.

John finds himself standing in . . . Heaven!

Above the atmosphere. Beyond the troposphere. Beyond the stratosphere. Beyond the mesosphere. Beyond the ionosphere. Beyond our solar system, beyond our galaxy, beyond the countless number of galaxies, beyond the innumerable stars. Far, far away beyond the universe.

So, how far did John travel?

Distances in the universe are so great that they have to be measured by the speed of light, which is 186,000 miles per second or 11,160,000 miles per minute. For example, our sun is about eight light minutes away. The Milky Way is 100,000 light years across and contains an estimated 100 billion stars. And it's only one of a billion known galaxies. The closest galaxy to ours is 200,000 light years away.

Traveling at the speed of light, we would leave Earth and reach Mercury, only 57 million miles away, in about four minutes and thirty seconds. To reach Jupiter, 390 million miles away, would take thirty-five minutes. Saturn, 793 million miles away, would take an hour and ten minutes. Uranus is 1.5 billion miles away, Neptune is 2.7 billion miles away, and Pluto a billion more.

But Heaven is even farther.

How long did it take John to travel through space and

reach Heaven? In the twinkling of an eye. Only God could have transported the apostle so far, so fast.

So John now finds himself standing in Heaven. One moment he was worshiping God on the island of Patmos, and the next he was in Heaven in the very presence of God.

What a trip!

TAKING DEAD AIM ON HEAVEN

Just as John made this dramatic trip to Heaven, God summons each one of us to make the same journey. Not just one day when we die, or when Christ returns. God desires that we turn our hearts toward Heaven now. In other words, we must preoccupy ourselves with Heaven.

Why focus upon Heaven?

Why read a book like this on Heaven?

C. S. Lewis said, "Aim at heaven and you will get earth thrown in. Aim at earth and you will get neither."[2] So what does aiming at Heaven afford us?

First, Heaven increases our knowledge of God. By looking to Heaven, we behold the full, unveiled manifestation of God's glory. Only in Heaven can we see His divine perfections most fully displayed. Heaven is where the glorified Christ dwells in holy light.

We must study Heaven in order to know our sovereign God and the glorified Christ more deeply. It is in Heaven that we see their full majesty and, correspondingly, grow in our personal knowledge of God.

A. W. Tozer said,

> To regain her lost power, the church must see Heaven opened and have a transforming vision of God. . . . Not the utilitarian God who is having a run of popularity today, whose chief claim to men's attention is His ability to bring them success in their various undertakings. . . . The God we must learn to know is the Majesty in the heavens. . . . He it is that sitteth upon the circle of the earth who stretcheth out the heavens as a curtain . . . who bringeth out His starry host by number and calleth them all by names through the greatness of His power,

*who seeth the works of man as vanity, who putteth no
confidence in princes and asks no counsel of kings.*[3]

Second, Heaven purifies our daily walk. The holy, sinless environment of Heaven calls us to live by the same
standard of personal holiness. The hope of Heaven cleans
out our hearts of inbred worldliness and alleviates sinful
living. John writes, "Everyone who has this hope fixed on
Him purifies himself, just as He is pure" (1 John 3:3).

For example, this summer my wife's parents came to
visit us—something they are rarely able to do. It was their
first visit to our new home, which we had recently bought.
Believe me, you can't imagine the time and effort that went
into cleaning our home before they arrived. Everything had
to be perfect. We dusted every piece of furniture, washed
every window, vacuumed every room, straightened up every
closet. Good grief, we even planted a new flower bed.

Why?

Because we wanted Anne's parents to be favorably
pleased with our new home.

I think this is analogous to what John is saying. The
hope of Heaven purifies us. Those who anticipate Christ's
coming and their going to Heaven will work hard at preparing themselves carefully. They will want God to be pleased
with the cleanliness of their lives. That's the positive motivation of Heaven.

Third, Heaven heals our broken hearts. Paul said that
the deepest pains of our wounded hearts are not worthy to
be compared with the glories to come (Romans 8:18). How
true! The more we gaze into Heaven, the more clearly we
understand that our present trials pale in comparison to the
glory that awaits us.

The Apostle Paul wrote,

*For all things are for your sakes, that the grace which is
spreading to more and more people may cause the giving
of thanks to abound to the glory of God. Therefore we do
not lose heart, but though our outer man is decaying,
yet our inner man is being renewed day by day. For*

*momentary, light affliction is producing for us an eternal
weight of glory far beyond all comparison.* (2 Corinthians
4:15-17)

What is your affliction today? Is it a strained relationship? A shattered dream? The disillusionment of a broken
marriage? The heartache of a prodigal child? Physical pain?

Then look to the glories of Heaven and be renewed in
your strength. When we consider the eternal weight of glory
that awaits us, we are filled with new hope. Knowing the
perfect comfort that awaits us in Heaven helps us endure
our present disappointments today.

Fourth, Heaven increases our motivation for evangelism. Focusing upon Heaven causes us to consider the eternal destinies of people more carefully. Heaven and hell
increase our burden to reach the lost with the saving gospel
of Jesus Christ. Because only personal faith in Jesus Christ
will usher sinful man into the presence of God, we are
gripped with a holy compulsion to witness for Christ now!
Heaven causes us to see all men in light of eternity.

Bottom line, we must take as many people with us to
Heaven as possible. Heaven causes us to think about cowork-
ers and neighbors who need Christ. Heaven forces us to
think about family members who need to be saved. These
people are perhaps only a heartbeat away from hell. We must
allow the reality of Heaven—that celestial dwelling place of
God—to energize and compel us to reach people with the
only message that ushers souls into God's presence.

Fifth, Heaven encourages our generosity in giving. The
more we live for Heaven, the more we will invest our
resources there. Jesus said, "Lay up for yourselves treasures
in Heaven, where neither moth nor rust destroys, and where
thieves do not break in or steal; for where your treasure is,
there will your heart be also" (Matthew 6:20-21). Heaven
calls us to be rich toward God and not stockpile goods here
on the earth. How's your giving? Where's your focus?

Sixth, Heaven brings an urgency to our ministry for
Christ. We have only so much time to serve Christ. What

24

we must do for Christ, we must do now. Heaven reminds us of the shortness of life here.

Jesus said, "I must work the works of Him who sent Me, as long as it is day; night is coming, when no man can work" (John 9:4). The night of eternity is coming soon when no man can work. So we must work while the day of opportunity burns brightly. Heaven and eternity await us sooner than we realize.

Jim Elliot is often quoted as having said, "One life to live, will soon be past. Only what's done for Christ will last."

Seventh, Heaven multiplies joy in our lives. The happiest Christians are those who focus upon Heaven. The psalmist writes, "In Thy presence is fulness of joy. In Thy right hand there are pleasures forevermore" (Psalm 16:11). Joy is to be found in Heaven now by anticipation and later by realization. Joyful are those people who have two feet upon the earth, but who breathe Heaven's air. If you would know deepest joy, then set your heart upon Heaven.

None of us can afford to neglect looking to Heaven. Nor can we fail to prepare ourselves for eternity. We must have a passion for the invisible world above where Christ is seated. Such a vision will radically transform our daily lives.

"He's so heavenly minded, he's no earthly good."

Don't bet on it.

Fact is, we're too worldly minded. Too earthbound. It is only those that are heavenly minded who become earthly good. May God significantly alter the direction of our lives today with a true vision of Heaven.

Heaven can't wait!

NOTES

1. John Piper, The Supremacy of God on Preaching (Grand Rapids, MI: Baker, 1990), pages 10-11.
2. Source unknown.
3. A. W. Tozer, The Knowledge of the Holy (San Francisco, CA: Harper and Row, 1961), pages 121-122.

Chapter Two

I'VE SEEN FIRE
AND I'VE SEEN REIGN

The Throne of Heaven

Revelation 4:2-8

⟆*ERSPECTIVE IS* EVERYTHING.

The higher you are, the better you see.

I was flying to Seattle for a Billy Graham Crusade when my flight took me over the majestic Rocky Mountains. As we approached the Washington Cascades, I was not prepared for the awesome sight I was about to see.

As if scripted by a Hollywood producer, my plane flew straight into a spectacular sunset that painted the surrounding mountain range a bright orange and fire-engine red. Before our pilot could make the announcement, I looked out my window and there it was. I was face-to-face with the most intimidating object I have ever seen—Mount Saint Helens.

Flying at 30,000 feet, even the imposing Rockies looked small. But this protruding peak towered above the earth, dwarfing even the mountain range. As we approached, I raised up in my seat as if our plane would scrape its belly on the top of the peak.

On May 18, 1980, volcanic power was unleashed from deep within this massive mountain and literally blew the top off, shaking the surrounding region with the force of an angry earthquake. Over 1,200 feet of the mountain exploded, spewing gas and debris some 63,000 feet into the atmosphere, leveling 3.2 billion feet of lumber. The surrounding landscape was instantly destroyed.

As our pilot sharply banked the plane over the open mouth of the volcano, I was now looking straight down the throat of this once fire-breathing monster. This gave me an entirely new perspective of its sheer majesty and awesome beauty. The setting sun reflected fiery colors off the snow-capped mountain peak, causing this monster to look alive again. Looking down from high above, Mount Saint Helens was incredible, awe-inspiring, and terrifying. Yet strangely beautiful.

What is even stranger is that years earlier I drove right past this colossal peak while on vacation. From ground level, I looked up and saw the mountain—but I thought nothing about it. The top half of the mountain was concealed above the clouds, so I could only see the base of the mountain. It looked like, well, any other mountain.

I had seen Mount Saint Helens before—but not like this. Only from this elevated position could I gain an entirely new perspective of this famous mountain peak. I had to be taken up to a high place before I could appreciate its raw majesty and heartstopping beauty.

Perspective is *everything*.

The higher you are, the better you see.

That's not just true with flying, but with life, as well. Some of us travel through life at ground level, seeing with only a limited, earthly perspective. Such people see only the bottom half of the mountain. But, to the contrary, others see life from a much different vantage point. They see from an elevated, heavenly perspective. They see the top half of the mountain protruding above the clouds. In reality, they see as God sees.

Where you stand determines what you see.

That's why we need to be taken up to Heaven in order to see life from an eternal perspective. We need to see above the clouds.

This is exactly what happened to the Apostle John. He was lifted up and enabled to see as God sees. He was summoned up to Heaven to gain an eternal perspective in order to see this world differently.

This is what it means to be heavenly minded. It means

to be so focused upon Heaven that one's perspective of earthly events is significantly changed. The person who is heavenly minded sets his mind on things above, not on things here below.

As you read this chapter, allow God to etch a vision of Heaven upon your heart. As you do, you will discover that the way you look at this life will be radically altered.

The Apostle John, imprisoned and confined on the Mediterranean island of Patmos, had a limited perspective. But God suddenly lifted him up and took him to Heaven, allowing him to see the unseen world of eternity. God called John to appear before His throne, saying, "Come up here" (Revelation 4:1). Immediately John was raptured, taken into the very throne room of Heaven. Only then could he see life from Heaven's perspective.

What exactly did John see?

THE AWESOME SIGHT
Once in Heaven, something immediately captures John's attention. The apostle is captivated by the single, most dominant feature in all Heaven. John sees a preeminent object standing at the epicenter of the vast, boundless Heaven.

Behold, a throne was standing in heaven. (Revelation 4:2)

John sees a throne—God's throne—standing erect in Heaven. God's throne is the center of the universe and the central theme of the book of Revelation. The throne of God is mentioned thirty-nine times in Revelation, thirteen times in Revelation 4. We could say that Revelation is the "throne book." And Revelation 4 is the "throne chapter."

Notice that John sees the throne *standing*. This divine seat of sovereignty is firmly set in place. Stable. Secure. Fixed. Established. Permanent. Immovable. Enduring. Eternal. It cannot be moved to another location for a lesser ruler to occupy. And it cannot be toppled by rival gods. This throne is standing erect and will remain forever in its rightful place.

The psalmist affirmed this when he said, "Thy throne,

O God, is forever and ever" (Psalm 45:6). God's throne towers over all earthly thrones, dwarfs all seats of human government, and presides over all creation.

Needless to say, this throne is the highest seat of absolute sovereignty. The seat of unchallenged, unrivaled authority. The chair of universal, global dominion. The place from which the galaxies are run. All creation—Heaven, earth, and even hell itself—must answer directly to this imposing throne. There is no higher court of appeal.

HE'S *STILL* ON THE THRONE!

John notices something further about this throne. He sees that it is not vacant, but occupied. Someone is enthroned upon it, and that Someone is God Himself.

> . . . *and One sitting on the throne.* (Revelation 4:2)

John actually—now get a grip on this—saw God sitting upon His throne! Can you imagine anything more glorious?

"Sitting" describes the position of a king who is actively reigning. For example, if a politician is *seated,* he is said to be in office. And if an elected official is put out of office, he is said to be *unseated.* John sees God *seated,* meaning He is actively exercising the duties of His executive office, administering over the affairs of all His creation.

Theologians call this the *visio dei*—the vision of God. The *visio* was the experience of Adam and Eve in Paradise as they walked in the light of God's undiminished glory. But since the Fall, sinful man has been denied that privilege, for as God told Moses, "No man can see Me and live!" (Exodus 33:20). The vision of God is the hope of all God's people as indicated in the priestly blessing, "The LORD make His face shine upon you . . . The Lord lift up His countenance on you" (Numbers 6:25-26). Seeing God is Jesus Christ's promise for all who will be made perfectly pure in Heaven. "Blessed are the pure in heart, for they shall see God" (Matthew 5:8). This vision was now John's experience—he saw *God!*

The message is clear to John. No matter what may happen

on earth, God is still on His throne in Heaven. God is still in control. He actively exercises His right to rule over all the universe. Here is the raw, sheer sovereignty of Almighty God revealed to John—and to us.

Regardless of earthly appearances, God has not been put out of office. He has not been unseated nor impeached. He is seated and in session, ruling and reigning over all the affairs of providence. Everything is under control because everything is under His control!

It was this same vision that the prophet Isaiah saw. Uzziah, Israel's long-seated king, had just died, and the nation was in crisis. A national crisis brewed. Who would succeed Uzziah? Who was in charge? As the nation mourned, the prophet came into the temple to seek God. It was while in the house of God that Isaiah received a sobering vision. He saw God Almighty seated in power.

The prophet writes, "In the year of King Uzziah's death, I saw the Lord sitting on a throne, lofty and exalted, with the train of His robe filling the temple" (Isaiah 6:1). Although Israel's throne was now vacant, Heaven's throne remained occupied.

Nebuchadnezzar, the proud king of Babylon, was seated upon his throne—until God put him out of office. Only then did Babylon's unseated king see Heaven's King seated upon His throne and say,

> *For His dominion is an everlasting dominion,*
> *And His kingdom endures from generation to generation.*
> *And all the inhabitants of the earth are accounted as*
>   *nothing,*
> *But He does according to His will in the host of heaven,*
> *And among the inhabitants of the earth;*
> *And no one can ward off His hand*
> *Or say to Him, "What hast Thou done?"* (Daniel 4:34-35)

In a similar context of adversity and affliction, the exiled Apostle John was given the same vision of God reigning in absolute sovereignty. How comforting and encouraging that must have been to be reminded that God was still on His throne.

At the time, John desperately needed this divine perspective. From his limited vantage point, Christianity was becoming a lost cause. By the end of the first century, it had been sixty long years since Pentecost, and the gospel enterprise had hardly become a world movement. Under the tyranny of Caesar, the Roman Empire was overshadowing and persecuting the early Church.

Hadn't Jesus promised the gates of Hades would not prevail against the Church (Matthew 16:18)? Didn't Jesus promise that John and the disciples would perform greater works than He (John 14:12)? Hadn't John heard it with his own ears?

But just the opposite seemed true. The Church was being persecuted. Her preachers killed. Her voice muzzled. Her progress stymied. Her witness all but snuffed out. It just wasn't happening. John must have wondered, *Where is God in all this?*

Have you ever asked that same question? I do just about every time I watch the evening news or read the newspaper. This world is sinking deeper and deeper into a quagmire of iniquity, while the cause of evangelical Christianity seems to be on the short end of the stick. The Church appears to be making less of an impact upon our culture, not more. High-profile preachers have fallen into sin. Other churches have stopped preaching the gospel altogether. Like salt that has lost its savor, the Church seems to be impotent.

I find myself asking, "God, are You still in control?"

As we see our world falling apart around us, we all must be reminded that God is doing something. He has not resigned. He has not been impeached. Nor put out of office. He's not even up for reelection. There are no term limits to His being God.

Have you looked up lately to see God still upon His throne? Have you come to understand that the events of your life are controlled by His sovereign throne? No matter what may seem out of control in your life, know that God is still in control.

Whatever your affliction, whatever your adversity, the truth of God's sovereignty is a healing balm. Stephen Charnock, the Puritan preacher wrote, "The throne of God drops honey and sweetness."[1]

Let us hear the poignant words of Charles H. Spurgeon again,

> *There is no attribute more comforting to His children than that of God's sovereignty. Under the most adverse circumstances, in the most severe trials, they believe that Sovereignty has ordained their afflictions, that Sovereignty overrules them and that Sovereignty will sanctify them all.*[2]

I believe that. He's still on His throne!

BLINDED BY THE LIGHT

There's more to the vision. John sees the effulgent glory of God, shining bright light from the throne, as though magnified through a perfect prism.

> *He who was sitting was like a jasper stone and a sardius in appearance.* (Revelation 4:3)

The ancient apostle struggles to describe what he sees. Finite language cannot describe the majesty of the infinite God. Using only the inadequate language of earth, the apostle describes God with human symbols in a frustrating attempt to communicate heavenly truth.

Jasper was a sparkling, crystal-clear stone, an opaque quartz of various colors (21:11). It was translucent, the most beautiful and precious gem. Moreover, it was known for its ability to refract light into a brilliant spectrum of vivid colors. So, as John sees God upon His throne, he sees bright colors and blinding light.

God's glory is like perfect light shining through a flawless gem. His sovereign majesty refracts all the beautiful colors of the spectrum. All this dazzling display of God's glory emanates from His throne. Blazing. Flashing. Shining.

Bright. Like the blinding radiance of the sun magnified by a perfectly cut, flawless, diamond-like prism.

Without any buffer or filter, John looks directly upon God's transcendent glory. He beholds His magnificent character. His holy radiance. His dazzling brilliance. His flashing splendor.

This bright light symbolizes God's absolute, unadulterated holiness. It pictures His flawless character, moral perfection, and unstained essence. Earlier John wrote, "God is light, and in Him there is no darkness at all" (1 John 1:5). Now he sees this divine light with his own eyes—and it's blinding!

What's more, John says that God is like a "sardius in appearance." The sardius stone was a fiery, deep red gem. A bright, glowing stone. The sardius reveals the fiery, red-hot wrath of God's fury. Apparently John was nearly blinded by the awesome glory surrounding the throne. The visual impact must have been overwhelming.

John sees God Himself enthroned. Ruling. Controlling. Pure. Holy. Blazing. Fiery. Wrathful. Brilliant. Glorious.

SOMEWHERE OVER THE RAINBOW

Second, John notes even more light—dazzling and brilliant—flashing around God's throne like a bright, beautiful rainbow. Completely encircling the throne is a circular green rainbow. Not an arch or half circle, but a complete circle. John continues:

> *And there was a rainbow around the throne, like an emerald in appearance.* (Revelation 4:3)

The astonished apostle sees a halo of emerald light surrounding the throne. Illuminated colored light stretches all around the throne, both above and below it. This resplendent, emerald-green rainbow testifies to God's perfect and complete grace, full and free, that is faithfully extended toward sinful man.

In Old Testament times, the rainbow represented God's faithfulness never to destroy the world again as He did with the flood (Genesis 9:13-15). It represented God's gracious covenant with His people. The unending rainbow the apostle describes means God's grace will endure forever.

Amid the white light of His holiness and the red flames of judgment, the green rainbow of God's grace shines brightly. In the midst of wrath, God remembers mercy. His grace triumphs over His judgment (James 2:13). It is His grace that prevents us from being consumed in the flames of His judgment.

Ezekiel saw the same celestial phenomenon: "As the appearance of the rainbow in the clouds on a rainy day, so was the appearance of the surrounding radiance. Such was the appearance of the likeness of the glory of the LORD" (Ezekiel 1:28). The prophet says that around God's throne is a rainbow-like radiance, the outshining of His grace and mercy.

Heaven remains the same to this day. This rainbow of mercy still arches and encircles over God's throne today—and it will forever! "The LORD's lovingkindnesses indeed never cease, for His compassions never fail. They are new every morning; great is Thy faithfulness" (Lamentations 3:22-23).

RESPECT YOUR ELDERS
John continues to peer into the throne room with captivating awe and amazement. Now he observes another facet of Heaven—twenty-four thrones around God's throne.

Around the throne were twenty-four thrones; . . . I saw twenty-four elders sitting, clothed in white garments, and golden crowns on their heads. (Revelation 4:4)

These are subsidiary thrones, subordinate to God's higher throne. They are lesser thrones with delegated authority, passed down from God Himself.

Ancient kings often surrounded their thrones with every form of pomp and ceremony to impress those brought before them. These lower thrones added to the dignity and awesomeness of the Sovereign's throne. Similarly,

God surrounds His heavenly throne with impressive regality and awe-inspiring majesty.

Upon these appellate thrones are seated twenty-four elders who share in God's reign. Who are these elders? The Greek word for elders is presbuteros, from which we get the English word Presbyterian.

I am reminded of the little girl who came home from her Presbyterian Sunday school, and her mother asked her what they had talked about.

"We talked about Heaven," the little girl replied.

"Well," her mother asked, "What did they say about it?"

"The teacher said only twenty-four Presbyterians made it to Heaven," the little girl said confidently.

(Hey, it's just a joke. We all know there won't be that many Presbyterians in Heaven.)

Some feel that these presbuteros are angelic beings, but I think not. More correctly, these are redeemed saints reigning in Heaven with Christ. The twenty-four elders represent the twelve tribes of Israel and the twelve apostles of the Church. Therefore, these twenty-four elders represent all the redeemed of all the ages who share in Christ's heavenly reign. Why do we say this?

First, these elders are seated upon thrones. In Heaven, redeemed saints are seen sitting upon thrones, but never angels (Revelation 20:4). Second, they are clothed in white garments, the garment of glorified believers in Heaven (3:5,18), not angels. Third, they are rewarded with crowns. Only believers are rewarded in Heaven, never angels (3:11). Fourth, they are called elders, something angels are never called. Fifth, they are twenty-four in number—an obvious reference to the twelve tribes of Israel and the twelve apostles of the Church that is hard to miss. Sixth, these elders are clearly distinguished from angels (4:11, 7:11). So, these elders represent all the redeemed from all the ages.

Why are elders seated upon thrones?

Because believers will reign with Christ and carry out important roles of judging, administrating, and overseeing (Revelation 20:4). Paul writes, "Do you not know that the saints will judge the world? . . . Do you not know that we shall judge angels?" (1 Corinthians 6:2-3).

Don't think that in Heaven we will be lying back on a bed of clouds, plucking harps, adjusting our halos, and singing "Kum Bah Ya." Personally, that sounds pretty boring to me. Heaven is an exciting place! A place of dynamic ministry, stimulating activity, and expanded horizons.

According to John's vision, we will be wearing white robes and golden crowns. White robes represent the imputed righteousness of Jesus Christ that makes a perfect covering for our sin (Revelation 3:5). At the same time, they also represent our good deeds done for Christ (Revelation 19:8). Golden crowns are eternal rewards given to us by Christ for faithful service in His Kingdom (1 Corinthians 9:24-25; 2 Timothy 4:8).

Will there be a white garment for you? Will you have a golden crown? How we live today determines the degree of our heavenly reward. Right now counts forever! Make your life count for eternity.

REIGN STORM

John observes another gripping component of this vision. He sees a threatening electrical storm brewing in Heaven and hears loud thunder booming from the throne. A terrifying storm is gathering a *reign* storm!

And from the throne proceed flashes of lightning and sounds and peals of thunder. (Revelation 4:5)

Swirling around God's throne is a destructive force ready to strike the earth. It is the full fury of God's wrath ready to be unleashed upon His enemies. Thunderbolts of divine anger are poised, ready to be hurled down in judgment upon this Christ-rejecting world.

The anger of God is building, ready to strike this sinful planet. God has prepared His throne for judgment. This gathering storm is reserved for the judgment of the final day.

Fast-forward ahead with me in Revelation and John describes this same violent storm in the seventh seal judgment. "And the angel took the censer; and he filled it with the fire of the altar and threw it to the earth; and there followed peals of thunder and sounds and flashes of lightning and an earthquake" (Revelation 8:5). Notice the same terminology, the same words, the same fury.

Likewise, the seventh trumpet judgment has the same lightning and thunder. "And the seventh angel sounded; and there arose loud voices in heaven. . . . And there were flashes of lightning and sounds and peals of thunder and an earthquake and a great hailstorm" (11:15,19). Again, same words, same fury. The exact image is used for the seventh bowl judgment (16:17-18).

So the seventh seal, trumpet, and bowl judgments comprise God's final wrath, ready to be poured out on this world at the end of the age. Right now, this terrible storm is brewing around God's throne; one day it will erupt upon this gospel-hardened earth.

Too many people have an aversion to the wrath of God. But holy vengeance is an indispensable aspect of His holy character. God could not be holy and, at the same time, be intolerant toward sin. He *must* punish sin.

The prophet writes,

> *A jealous and avenging God is the LORD.*
> *The LORD is avenging and wrathful.*
> *The Lord takes vengeance on His adversaries,*
> *And He reserves wrath for His enemies.*
> *The LORD is slow to anger and great in power,*
> *And the Lord will by no means leave the guilty*
>   *unpunished. . . .*
> *Who can stand before His indignation?*
> *Who can endure the burning of His anger?*
> *His wrath is poured out like fire.* (Nahum 1:2-3,6)

HEAVEN ON FIRE!

When we think of hell, we think of burning fire. But have you considered the burning fires of Heaven? Consider what John sees next. He sees seven burning lamps flickering and dancing before God's throne.

*There were seven lamps of fire burning before the throne,
which are the seven Spirits of God.* (Revelation 4:5)

Seven lamps of fire—literally, torches—are smoldering
before God's throne. These are not small lamps, the kind we
might use indoors by which to read, but large torches that
light up the vast outdoors. In the Old Testament, such
torches were used to signify that God was ready to expose
His enemies and make war (Judges 11, Nahum 2). These
blazing lamps illumine the landscape of Heaven.

These burning torches represent the Holy Spirit (Revelation 1:4). There are not seven Holy Spirits, but one Spirit
(Ephesians 4:4). These flames represent the multifaceted,
complete ministry of the third member of the Trinity. This
sevenfold work of the Spirit was described in Isaiah 11:2 as
(1) the Spirit of the Lord, (2) the spirit of wisdom, (3) the
spirit of understanding, (4) the spirit of counsel, (5) the spirit
of strength, (6) the spirit of knowledge, and (7) the spirit of
the fear of the Lord.

In the Bible, the Holy Spirit is often pictured as fire. Like
a burning fire, the Holy Spirit illumines, enlightens, warms,
burns, empowers, energizes, purifies, melts down, and con-
sumes. Fire symbolizes the ever-active, all-wise, all-seeing
Holy Spirit. He is always ready to illumine and empower the
righteous and, at the same time, consume the wicked.

This imagery of fires recalls the words of John the Baptist, who proclaimed the coming of the Holy Spirit's
judgment.

> *"I baptize you with water for repentance, but He who is
> coming after me is mightier than I, and I am not fit to
> remove His sandals; He will baptize you with the Holy
> Spirit and fire. And His winnowing fork is in His hand,
> and He will thoroughly clear His threshing floor; and He
> will gather His wheat into the barn, but He will burn up
> the chaff with unquenchable fire."* (Matthew 3:11-12)

The Holy Spirit will consume every unbeliever in the
final judgment. The Comforter will become the Consumer!

The prophet Ezekiel wrote, "In the midst of the living beings there was something that looked like burning coals of fire, like torches darting back and forth among the living beings. The fire was bright, and lightning was flashing from the fire"(Ezekiel 1:13). These leaping flames are the Holy Spirit, representing His perfect purity. He is the *Holy* Spirit! Fire not only makes pure, it *is* pure.

So around God's throne is the brilliant fire of the Holy Spirit, burning like seven torches—the purging fire of His purity and wrath. What John is telling us is, "I've seen fire, and I've seen reign!"

CRYSTAL LIGHT

The bewildered eyes of John, awestruck in amazement, continue to scan the incredible scene of Heaven. Next he sees a massive crystal sea solidified beneath God's throne.

And before the throne there was, as it were, a sea of glass like crystal. (Revelation 4:6)

Here is a massive ocean, like perfect, crystal-like glass, under God's throne. This glistening gulf refracts the bright shining glory of God, reflecting its light throughout Heaven. It is a pavement of pure, solid crystal on which God's throne rests.

Picture the beauty of this scene! A brilliant rainbow and the flashing colors of emerald green, sardius red, and jasper white all splashing off this sea of crystal! Bright colors and blinding light are all magnified exponentially through a pure, crystal sea, each hue displaying the infinite splendor of God's throne.

Each summer, my wife, Anne, our four children, and I travel to Florida for our family vacation. Let me tell you, the August sun is blinding in Florida—especially at the beach. The shining ocean and white sand reflect the sun's rays, magnifying its brightness. The sun is so bright, I have to squint even with sunglasses on.

That's precisely the effect of the crystal sea in Heaven. It serves to multiply and magnify the full intensity of the dazzling display of God's blinding glory. In John's vision, all Heaven is literally ablaze with the bright radiance of His holy character.

Moses described this same glass pedestal beneath God's throne. "They saw the God of Israel; and under His feet there appeared to be a pavement of sapphire, as clear as the sky itself" (Exodus 24:10). Wow! Think about it—a highway of clear sapphire as far as you can see, upholding God's throne.

Ezekiel also described it, "Now over the heads of the living beings there was something like an expanse, like the awesome gleam of crystal, extended over their heads" (Ezekiel 1:22). Above the angels and below the throne, a crystal-clear expanse—dazzling, awesome, gleaming—stretching clear across the sky.

The architecture of Heaven is theocentric, designed for one thing—to reflect and magnify the brilliant glory of God.

Talk about a light show! Here is God's laser show, showing off His glory for all the universe to see. No wonder the angels cover their faces.

BEAUTY AND THE BEASTS
Finally, John sees four living creatures in the immediate vicinity of God's throne. These creatures are encircling the throne on all four sides.

> *In the center and around the throne, four living creatures full of eyes in front and behind. And the first creature was like a lion, and the second creature like a calf, and the third creature had a face like that of a man, and the fourth creature was like a flying eagle. And the four living creatures, each one of them having six wings, are full of eyes around and within; and day and night they do not cease to say, "HOLY, HOLY, HOLY, is THE LORD GOD, the ALMIGHTY, who was and who is and who is to come.*
> (Revelation 4:6-8)

Here are four living creatures—literally, four living *beings*—flying around God's throne. These are angelic beings, probably cherubim, in the immediate vicinity of the throne, forming an inner circle of worshipers.

The prophet Ezekiel clearly identifies them as cherubim, a separate order of angels. He writes, "Then the cherubim rose up. They are the living beings that I saw. . . . These are the living beings that I saw beneath the God of Israel by the river Chebar; so I knew that they were cherubim" (Ezekiel 10:15,20). Cherubim are the highest order of angelic beings, with special proximity to the throne. They are a privileged class of exalted angels from whose ranks Satan, the highest of all angels, fell (28:14,16).

Cherubim are not plump, naked, baby angels, shooting people with Cupid-like arrows of love. Quite the contrary, they function as powerful guardians who stand at the divine throne, guarding the holiness of God. In much the same way, they protected the tree of life in the Garden of Eden. Now they do the same in Heaven, controlling access to the throne.

They have "eyes in front and behind," indicating their conscious awareness, comprehensive knowledge, constant vigilance, penetrating intelligence, clear insight, mental alertness, and clear discernment. Like a lion, ox, man, and eagle, these angelic beings have great strength, humble servanthood, insightful wisdom, and swift speed to carry out God's agenda. They possess relentless drive and powerful wills in serving God.

Isaiah's description of the seraphim suggests why. Much like cherubim, seraphim are another special order of angels having close proximity to the throne of God. Isaiah states, "With two he covered his face, and with two he covered his feet; and with two he flew" (Isaiah 6:2). Two wings cover their faces, denoting their awe of God lest they look upon Him in His blinding glory. Two wings cover their feet, denoting their deep humility because they stand on holy ground and with two wings they fly, symbolizing their readiness and swift mobility in order to obey God's commands immediately.

Finally, John observes endless praise directed to the throne of God. Day and night these cherubim offer constant worship to God upon His throne. They offer unending tribute to God, the Almighty.

A HIGH VIEW OF GOD

This vision *must* greatly impact our lives today. We *must* be gripped with this high view of God. We *must* elevate our thoughts of Him.

Being heavenly minded means that our lives are dominated and driven by such a vision of God.

When we see God upon His throne, we can only conclude that no sacrifice is too great to offer Him. No pursuit is too small to be conducted independently of Him. No decision is to be made without Him.

An American pastor traveled to the Far East and, while there, took a guided tour of a large Buddhist temple.

As he walked through the religious shrine, he noticed the luxurious furnishings, the lavish fixtures, and the costly materials that had all gone into making this ornate temple. It was more plush than any house of worship he had ever seen before. He was, well, overwhelmed!

Turning to the tour guide, the pastor asked, "Do you mind if I ask you a question? How much did it *cost* to build this temple?"

As if insulted, the Buddhist tour guide stopped in his tracks and replied, "*Cost? What cost?* We don't think of cost when it comes to Buddha."

Then, leaning closer to the pastor, the tour guide said, "Sir, you must understand. *There is nothing* too good for Buddha."

A high view of their god—a false god, at that—had driven them to make whatever sacrifice necessary to worship their lifeless idol. Because they perceived their deaf mute, inanimate god to be so great, there could be no cost cutting in worshiping him.

Shouldn't the same be true with us—but on a much greater scale? We alone know and serve the one true God. Our God is the living God. He alone is enthroned in Heaven in glory and majesty. And there is nothing too good for *our* God.

What an indictment against our casual Christianity that wants to give God our leftovers, our second best, our hand-me-downs. Our God deserves the greatest sacrifice of our lives, because He is enthroned on high.

Like the old gospel song says, "It won't be old Buddha who's sitting on the throne. And it won't be old Mohammed that's calling us home. And it won't be Hare Krishna who plays that trumpet tune, Cause we're going to see the Son, not Reverend Moon."[3]

Only our God is the living God. He alone deserves our best. He alone deserves our all. Bottom line, nothing is too good for our God.

No cost is too high to pay. No commitment is too deep to make. No sacrifice is too great to offer.

Give God your best. Whatever you are doing, wherever you are, whoever you are with—give God your best!

Nothing is too great for our God—*nothing!*

NOTES

1. Stephen Charnock, *The Existence and Attributes of God*, vol. 2 (Grand Rapids, MI: Baker, 1979), page 449.

2. Charles H. Spurgeon, *The New Park Street Pulpit*, vol. 2 (Pasadena, TX: Pilgrim Publications, 1981), page 185.

3. "Oh Buddha" by Mark Farrow, © 1993, Word Music. Used by permission.

Chapter Three

THE CROWD'S ON THEIR . . . *FACE!*

The Worship of Heaven
(Part One)

Revelation 4:8-11

T̶HE PLACE WAS ALIVE!

Never have I been anywhere so emotionally charged—
never! The crowd was delirious. Stomping feet. Clapping
hands. High fiving. Back slapping. Yelling. Hugging. Waving. Dancing. Screaming. Jumping. And the game hadn't
even started yet.

Chicago Stadium was about to witness another epic per-
formance by the greatest athlete of our time, the biggest
icon in all sports—Michael Jordan. What a way to celebrate
my twin boys' tenth birthday!

For over an hour, diehard fanatics stood in line, waiting
for the gates to open, just to cheer on their beloved Bulls.
When the gates opened, over sixteen thousand people
jammed into every square inch of the stadium. Not to mention another three thousand diehards who paid for the privilege to stand in the outer aisles of the nosebleed section
known as the upper balconies.

Unquestionably, courtside was the place to be. The red-
bordered hardwood was crawling with high-profile celebrities, corporate moguls, big-time entertainers, and the social
elite. Everyone was upbeat. Expectant. Happy. Cameras were
flashing. Television cameras rolling. Lights glaring.

The place was *alive!*

Announcing the starting lineups was a religious experience. The visiting Charlotte Hornets were introduced first.

And the hometown crowd gave the visiting team the emotional feedback of a wax museum.

Suddenly the stadium lights were cut off and the entire coliseum turned pitch dark. Then, projected onto the ceiling above, a psychedelic laser show flashed across the arena, lighting up the crowd. *Star Wars* music thundered in the background. *Yes!*

As the Bulls were introduced, the arena got so loud I couldn't even hear myself think. My ears were "bleeding." I had goose bumps that were high-fiving each other.

As the house lights were turned back on, a military flag guard marched out to center court bearing the American flag. Background music began to play and a young woman walked out to sing the national anthem. Listen, she could have raised the dead with her punched-up rendition of "The Star Spangled Banner." As she sang the last lines, the crowd did the impossible—they drowned out her piercing voice with their standing O.

The place was *alive!*

And the game hadn't even started yet.

With multiplied millions watching coast-to-coast via cable television, Michael Jordan—the human highlight film—lit up the scoreboard with one of the greatest games of his storied career. *Fifty-two* points!

By the end of the game, the crowd was *really* delirious. Celebrating D-Day must have seemed calm in comparison. The place was bedlam. Stomping. Clapping. Yelling. Waving. Dancing. Screaming. Jumping. When the final buzzer sounded, nobody left. Everyone just stayed, basking in the glory of the moment. Why leave a happening, for pity's sake?

That was *Friday*.

Sunday was another story.

On Sunday morning, I took my boys to the worship service of a church in the greater Chicago area. Unfortunately, it was a totally different scene from the one we witnessed Friday night. We just weren't prepared for how different.

With the excitement of the Bulls' game still reverberating in our minds, we purposefully arrived at church fifteen

49

minutes early, just to make sure that we could get a good seat. Or maybe just to *find* a seat—any seat. Our taxi dropped us off at the sanctuary's front door and we hurried into the worship center, ready to fight the crowd. As we bolted through the doors leading into the sanctuary, we were hit with a startling surprise.

Thousands of worshipers were *not* waiting for the front doors of the church to be opened. People were *not* standing three-deep around the outer aisles. People were *not* jammed into every square inch of the sanctuary.

The place was virtually *empty*.

The bottom floor was half full—*barely*.

We easily got three seats together—right smack dab in the center of the front row. We had the pick of any seat in the house. No problem. You could have fired a cannon in that massive sanctuary and not hit a soul.

The service itself was an exercise in boredom. The bland leading the bland. The soloist droned on with the excitement level you feel when standing in line to get your car tags renewed. The missions speaker wore a South American native costume, taught us a chorus in Spanish (now that's relevant), and basically filibustered until noon.

When the pastor pronounced the closing benediction, the place emptied faster than a bathtub with a leak.

Talk about a contrast!

On Friday night, multiplied *thousands* were jammed in to watch Michael Jordan dribble a zipped up leather bag of air. But Sunday morning, only a few *hundred* were scattered around in a large sanctuary to worship the Sovereign Ruler of Heaven and earth. One night, *multitudes* cheered for the world champions; but hours later, only a *handful* even showed up to acknowledge the world's Creator.

What's wrong with this picture?

People excited about Michael Jordan, but bored with Jesus Christ?

This world is so backwards. Upside-down. Inverted. Flip-flopped. Opposite. Those two scenes should have been reversed. Nineteen thousand die-hards should have been jammed in to worship the *Lamb*—not the *Bulls*. There should have been a traffic jam to see *Jehovah*—not *Jordan*.

EMPTY CHURCHES, EMPTY HEARTS

Something's missing. I don't know *when* we lost it. But it's definitely gone. A deep sense of worship in the church has been lost—a sense of reverence, awe, celebration, excitement, and joy. Why? I believe we've lost our vision of the Almighty. We need to recapture a glorious vision of the resplendent majesty of our Sovereign Lord reigning above. When we do, our worship of God will be restored.

Too many believers are just plain *bored* in their Christian life and *bored* in their worship of God. The problem is, our concept of God is too small. We act like God can't even "slam dunk" as well as Michael Jordan. Only when we see the true God—the enthroned God of Heaven—will our hearts respond with fervent praise and deep devotion.

In this chapter, we will discover what true worship looks and sounds like. Believe me, it's anything but boring. If we are to recapture dynamic worship in our hearts, we must first recapture a vision of the true God.

This is the heart of what it means to be heavenly minded. It means to set our minds on God above; then we will know what it is to worship as the angels and glorified saints. The one who is truly heavenly minded is, first and foremost, an intent worshiper of God.

What is worship? It is honor and adoration being directed toward God. Worship is ascribing to God His worth or affirming His supreme value. It is a consuming, selfless desire to give God His due, which is the sacrifice of our hearts, our praise, our obedience, our possessions. In short, our very lives. Bottom line, worship is living every moment of every day to glorify God.

As we look at the worship of Heaven, we discover several features that should distinguish our worship here and now. In Revelation 4:8-11, the scene around God's throne is genuine worship distinguished by a declaration of His greatness (verse 8), a celebration of His goodness (verse 9), a submission before His sovereignty, adoration of His eternality, and self-renunciation before His throne (verse 10), and an exaltation of His sovereignty (verse 11).

May these components of heavenly worship be present in our earthly lives!

WHOLLY, WHOLLY HOLY

First, worship involves a declaration of His greatness. Here is the worship by the angels, as recorded by John, in which the host of Heaven declare the greatness of God.

> *The four living creatures, each one of them having six wings, are full of eyes around and within; and day and night they do not cease to say, "HOLY, HOLY, HOLY, IS THE LORD GOD, THE ALMIGHTY, who was and who is and who is to come.* (Revelation 4:8)

These heavenly creatures—literally, "living ones"—are angelic beings. According to Ezekiel 10:20, these are the cherubim—angelic attendants around God's throne who serve as guardians of His holiness, composing the highest order of the angelic population.

What are these cherubim doing? They are doing what they were created to do—they are worshiping the living God. They offer incessant praise, continuous worship, and unending tribute to God. Certainly this does not preclude other heavenly duties and cosmic functions. While worship is not their sole activity, it is their chief priority.

These angelic worshipers in Heaven adore God first for His holiness. Day and night the heavenly host is crying out "HOLY, HOLY, HOLY" (Revelation 4:8).

If holiness is this important—and it is—then what does it mean? Can we get a handle on God's holiness? Absolutely.

The essential meaning of holy is "separate" or "separateness." The word is derived from a Semitic root meaning "to cut, to separate," like someone cutting an object in half so as to separate the two halves. Literally, holiness means that something or someone is cut apart and separated.

Specifically, the word *holy* is used in two different ways.

That is, it carries both a primary and secondary meaning. First, holiness means that God is a cut above us, infinitely transcendent, above and beyond His creation. In other words, He is totally distinct from us. Unique. One of a kind. We cannot compare Him with anyone or anything here, because He vastly exceeds all comparisons.

Isaiah wrote, "To whom then will you liken God? Or what likeness will you compare with Him?" (Isaiah 40:18). These are rhetorical questions implying the negative answer—*no one*! He is exalted in holiness! God is so elevated above all His creation that no comparison can even be made between Him and us. The chasm is *infinite!*

The second meaning of God's holiness is moral purity. This means He is free from any stain of sin and is wholly perfect. God is morally sinless and never does anything wrong—*never!* He *never* errs. He *never* makes a misjudgment. He never causes something to happen that isn't right. Like a flawless diamond, God is utterly, absolutely perfect.

The holiness of God demands that He judge sin. He has a holy hatred of sin that cannot tolerate any unrighteousness. He cannot skip over sin. Instead, His holiness demands that He pour out His fierce wrath upon everything that does not conform to His perfect character.

With intentional repetition, the angels echo this ascription of greatness three times—*holy, holy, holy*. This means that God is holy to the supreme or superlative degree. In English we express degree by saying that something is good, better, or best. The Hebrew would express the same emphasis by repeating the word. To repeat a word three times meant the superlative degree—it was the very best. Unsurpassed. Thus, "holy, holy, holy" means that God is holy, holier, holiest. In other words, He is the holiest Being in all the universe.

The angels are not crying out, "Love, love, love," although God certainly is infinite love. Nor are they saying, "Grace, grace, grace," although God surely is full of grace. Rather, they are saying, "Holy, Holy, Holy." Holiness is the one attribute of God raised to the highest degree.

This should not surprise us, because holiness—more

53

than any other divine attribute—captures the true essence of who God is. It is the centerpiece of His attributes.

A Ruler Without Measure

The angels are also praising God for *His sovereignty*. This One who is holy is none other than "THE LORD GOD" (Revelation 4:8).

Lord is the key word here. This title for God (*kurios*) means "sovereign Ruler, absolute Master, ruling Potentate." As the Lord God, He alone possesses the right to rule. His throne is the highest authority. His will is unrivaled and supreme. He has authority to do *whatever* He pleases, *whenever* He pleases, with *whomever* He pleases. The psalmist confirms, "Our God is in the heavens; He does whatever He pleases" (Psalm 115:3).

God's sovereignty means that He has absolute control over all of His creation. God causes *some* things to happen; He allows *other* things to happen; but He controls all things. Nothing happens apart from His sovereignty.

Clothed with absolute sovereignty, God alone possesses the divine prerogative to rule over the affairs of men, to govern our circumstances, and to determine our eternal destinies. The Apostle Paul writes, "For from Him and through Him and to Him are all things" (Romans 11:36). As the Source, all things are from Him. As the Means, all things are through Him. As God, all things are for Him. He is Architect, Builder, and Owner of all things.

God's sovereignty extends even to the eternal destinies of men. Paul writes,

> *Does not the potter have a right over the clay, to make from the same lump one vessel for honorable use, and another for common use? What if God, although willing to demonstrate His wrath and to make His power known, endured with much patience vessels of wrath prepared for destruction? And He did so in order that He might make known the riches of His glory upon vessels of mercy, which He prepared beforehand for glory.* (Romans 9:21-23)

54

This will be one of the primary aspects of our worship in Heaven—our response to the sovereignty of God. All who appear before God's throne in eternity will know that they are there as a result of His choice. Each of us will be filled with a deep humility and wonder in His presence: "Why me, Lord? Why me?"

Let us never forget this lesson. God is the Potter, we are the clay. He molds and fashions us as He wills. He turns the wheel of providence and shapes our destinies as it pleases Him best. He makes us and breaks us, forms us and conforms us, as He determines. All our times are in His hand.

No Power Shortage

Further, the angels in Heaven are praising God for *His omnipotence*. He is declared to be God "THE ALMIGHTY" (Revelation 4:8). This means that He is all-powerful. There is no power that exists outside of Himself. His power knows no limits. There is nothing He cannot do. He uses His power to accomplish His perfect will with absolute ease.

God never grows weary or becomes tired. He never loses any power. He never has to strain or push Himself to accomplish His will. Nothing is too hard for the Almighty.

Because God is the Almighty, all power comes from Him. The only power that men or angels possess is derived from God. He possesses absolute power over nature, Satan, demons, circumstances, life, illness, and death.

Worship is precisely what occurred after the Israelites passed safely through the Red Sea. In response to the display of God's power, Moses and the people burst into songs of praise, "I will sing to the LORD, for He is highly exalted. The horse and its rider He has hurled into the sea. The LORD is my strength and song; and He has become my salvation . . .; the LORD is a warrior; the LORD is His name. Pharaoh's chariots and his army He has cast into the sea" (Exodus 15:1-4).

He Just Keeps Going, and Going . . .

God is praised by the angels for *His eternality*. He is "THE LORD GOD who was and who is and who is to come" (Revelation 4:8).

God is eternal. There has never been a time in the past when God was not. There will never be a time in the future when God will not be. He has always existed in eternity past and will continue to do so for all eternity future. He always was, and He always will be.

The psalmist writes, "Even from everlasting to everlasting, Thou art God" (Psalm 90:2). That's God—from eternity past to eternity future.

When the earth was created, God had already existed, millions and billions of years. There has never been a time when God did not exist. Never.

God alone is the uncreated One. He is the original first cause of which everything else is the effect. He is the Creator who was before anything else was. He existed before the foundation of the world, eternally preexistent. He predates time and precedes all that there is because He is the God who was.

Likewise, He is the God "who is"—meaning that He dwells in the present—and He is our God "who is to come"—meaning He will continue to exist as God throughout all eternity future. In the ages to come, God will always be God. Never to be impeached. Never to be succeeded.

God is always previous. He dwells beyond time in one eternal present. He stands with one foot in eternity past and the other foot in eternity future and spans all of time. What He planned previously in eternity past He executes presently within time, and He will bring to its appointed end in eternity future.

God Is Not Codependent

The angels are praising God because of *His self-existence.* As the God "who is," He depends on nothing outside of Himself to exist. He needs nothing outside of Himself to be Himself. He is totally complete within Himself.

This is how God identified Himself to Moses, "WHO I AM" (Exodus 3:14). The Lord said to Moses, "Thus, you shall say to the sons of Israel, 'I AM has sent me to you.'" It is from this divine name that YHWH is derived. YHWH, rendered

"LORD," comes from the Hebrew verb hayah, meaning "to be." Yahweh is.

His self-existence is not too complicated to understand. It simply means He depends on no one or nothing else for His existence. God was never codependent. He simply is.

As the independent, self-existent, self-generating God, He is all and in all (Colossians 3:11). He upholds all, provides for all, maintains all, watches over all, guides all, and directs all. All by Himself.

I was speaking in a church recently, and a man gave a word of testimony before I preached. In his message, this man said something that greatly blessed my heart. Enthusiastically, he said, "God is God—all by Himself."

That's right! The angels are praising God because He is God—all by Himself!

Forever the Same!

Finally, the angels are praising God for *His immutability*. He is "THE LORD GOD who was and who is and who is to come" (Revelation 4:8).

These three descriptions linking together God past, present, and future signify God's unchangableness. The God who "was" is the God who "is," and the God who "was and is" is the God who "is to come." He never changes! He never increases to the good nor diminishes to the bad. He is eternally the same.

Every aspect about God is unchanging. He is changeless in His character. Changeless in His will. Changeless in His Word. This world changes. Culture changes. Society changes. Fashions change. The weather changes. People change. But God never changes.

The psalmist wrote,

Of old Thou didst found the earth;
And the heavens are the work of Thy hands.
Even they will perish, but Thou dost endure;
And all of them will wear out like a garment;

Like clothing Thou will change them,
    and they will be changed.
But Thou art the same,
And Thy years will not come to an end. (Psalm 102:25-27)

The prophet Malachi declared, "For I, the LORD, do not change; therefore you, O sons of Jacob, are not consumed" (3:6).

The New Testament teaches, "Every good thing bestowed and every perfect gift is from above, coming down from the Father of lights, with whom there is no variation, or shifting shadow" (James 1:17). Immutability uniquely sets God apart because all His creation is constantly changing. All change is either for the better or for the worse, but any change is inconceivable with God. The Lord couldn't be any better, and He wouldn't be any worse. He never changes.

Never.

The hymn goes, "We blossom and flourish as leaves on the tree, and wither and perish but naught changeth Thee." This is the God the angels worship. This is the God glorified saints worship in Heaven. Is this the God you worship?

This lofty knowledge of God must infect our worship with godly zeal. Low thoughts of God will breed callous worship. But a high view of God inflames us with fervent worship.

Have you lost your vision of such a high view of God?

It is essential that we elevate our view of God. We must have high, lofty, noble thoughts of God. Let us worship His holiness. Let us fall down before His sovereignty. Let us boast in His omnipotence. Let us magnify His eternality. Let us rejoice in His self-existence. Let us exult in His immutability.

Behold your God!

One more point. Notice that the Scripture says here, "They do not cease to say. . . ." Don't miss this! These angels do more than know the attributes of God. They declare them. They constantly boast—verbally—in God.

What about you? Is His greatness always on your lips?

CELEBRATE! CELEBRATE!

Second, worship is a celebration of His goodness. Worship is, essentially, the heartfelt response of those in the presence of God to His glory, especially to His goodness.

> *And when the living creatures give glory and honor and thanks to Him who sits on the throne, to Him who lives forever and ever.* (Revelation 4:9)

Those in Christ's presence give Him glory. There are two aspects of God's glory. First, there is what we might call His intrinsic glory—the glory which is the sum total of the outshining of all His divine perfection. It is the intrinsic essence of God that shines out for us to see.

Moses longed to see God's radiant, essential glory when he said, "I pray Thee; show me Thy glory!" (Exodus 33:18). It was this very glory the angels proclaimed (Isaiah 6:3), Jesus revealed (John 1:14), and Stephen preached (Acts 7:2).

Second, there is the glory that is given to God—the glory that is expressed here in this worship scene. This glory is the honor that men and angels render to the Lord Himself. The rightful recognition of His greatness that belongs to God alone.

This is man's supreme purpose—to give glory to God. He created us to worship Him and honor His name.

Such celebration is what the psalmist invites us to participate in.

> *Shout joyfully to the LORD, all the earth.*
> *Serve the LORD with gladness;*
> *Come before Him with joyful singing. . . .*
> *Enter His gates with thanksgiving,*
> *And His courts with praise.*
> *Give thanks to Him; bless His name.* (Psalm 100:1-2,4)

This must be the joyful experience of our hearts. This must be the expression of our hearts.

Let me address something here. Many well-educated unbelievers, and even some thinking Christians, have noticed a supposed problem with all this worship. Their reasoning goes something like this: "If God requires all these people to be telling Him how great He is all the time, He must be totally insecure. But if God is insecure, then He surely doesn't deserve our worship." This conclusion reveals a misunderstanding about the true nature of God. A comprehensive view of God from the Scriptures reveals that He does not need our worship. There is nothing lacking in God. Just the opposite; we are the ones who need to worship Him.

The Bible presents God as complete in Himself, lacking in nothing. He didn't create us because He was lonely and needed fellowship. Rather, He fashioned us in His image in such a way that if we fail to worship Him, then we are incomplete and lacking. It is only in our worship of Him that we find true fulfillment and satisfaction. The choice to worship God is in our best interest.

Praise His name!

HOW LOW CAN YOU GO?
Third, worship requires our submission before His sovereignty. All worship involves our utter humility before God. No one struts haughtily into the presence of God. All who come into His holy presence are struck with a deep, profound sense of their own unworthiness as they approach the throne. The closer we draw to God, the more we are struck with awe and amazement.

> *The twenty-four elders will fall down before Him who sits on the throne.* (Revelation 4:10)

Joining in with the angels' adoration is the worship of all the redeemed saints in Heaven. The elders—representing all the saved of all the ages—now respond to the worship of the cherubim and join with them in praising God. Worship is always contagious—always! Perhaps it is the angels' greater proximity to the throne that leads John to record their worship first. As his eye scopes this scene, his sight moves away from the throne to these elders who immediately surround these angels.

If the angels reveal to us who we worship, the elders show us how to worship. We are not surprised to find these worshipers flat on their faces before God. People in the presence of God always fall down before Him. Seeing the unveiled glory of God always pulls the rug out from under prideful people and puts them belly down on their faces.

We learn here that true worship is never giddy. Never shallow, superficial, or flippant. I have heard young people sing, "Jesus is the salt on my Frito." I have heard of worship leaders stepping into the pulpit with a loud Mickey Mouse tie—trivializing the transcendent. No wonder our worship is so Goofy! Listen, these things ought not to be. Where is our reverence?

God's people should always worship Him with a broken heart and a contrite spirit. The only authentic response to beholding God's holiness is humility.

Isn't that what we feel when we genuinely worship God? Unworthiness? Humility? Brokenness? Between God's holiness and our unholiness is a gulf that can only be bridged by God's grace. Until we understand the holiness of God, we can never know the depth of our own sinfulness. We will be shaken down to the core of our very being every time we see ourselves in comparison to Him.

I read about a man who was walking through an art gallery when he came upon a picture of Jesus Christ dying upon the cross. He stopped and looked at the beautiful portrait of Calvary's love.

As he stared into the face of Christ, so full of agony, the gallery guard tapped him on the shoulder. "Lower," the guard said. "The artist painted this picture to be appreciated from a lower position."

So the man bent down. And from this lower position, he observed new beauties in the picture previously not seen. But the guard interrupted him again.

"Lower," he said. "Lower still."

The man knelt down on one knee and looked up into the face of Christ. The new vantage point yielded new beauties to behold and appreciate.

But motioning with his flashlight toward the ground, the attendant said, "Lower. You've got to go lower."

The man now dropped down to two knees and looked up. Only then, as he looked up at the painting from such a low posture could he realize the artist's intended perspective. Only then could he see the full beauty of the Cross.

The same is true in worship. Only as we posture ourselves lower and lower in humble submission can we behold more fully the glories of Christ's majesty. Let us humble ourselves in His holy presence—yet lower and lower still—until we fall flat on our face in His presence. Only then will we experience true worship.

COME, LET US ADORE HIM
Fourth, worship involves the adoration of His person. These elders, John writes, worship God with deep adoration.

> *And will worship Him who lives forever and ever.*
> (Revelation 4:10)

The word worship (*proskuneo*) means "to kiss toward, to kiss the hand, to bow down." It means to bow before a sovereign ruler in humble adoration. It means to ascribe "worth-ship" to something or someone. Thus, worship is recognizing and responding to who God is and affirming His supreme value.

In ancient times, when a subject would approach his king, he would come in great submission and humility with head bowed low. The king would extend his hand upon which he wore the royal signet ring. This ring symbolized all the sovereignty and regal majesty of the king's throne.

The subject would then kiss the ring, and by doing so he would pay homage and respect and, at times, even worship to the king. This is the imagery upon which this Greek word is based.

When we talk about worship, we are talking about something we give to God. It is an all-consuming, selfless desire to give to God our lives, our praise, our possessions, our attitudes, our all.

Think of the magi who came to worship the Christ-Child. These oriental king makers picture for us the true essence of worship. They came into the presence of the holy Child, fell down before Him, and gave Him gifts. Costly, valuable gifts of gold, frankincense, and myrrh. Gifts befitting a king.

These Christ-worshipers demonstrated their adoration by giving Him gifts. No worshiper can come empty-handed into His presence. Worship is all about giving—not getting. It's all about giving Him praise, giving Him glory, giving Him our gifts, giving Him our lives (Romans 12:1).

Only in giving do we receive. Only as we give glory to Christ do we receive back from Him the grace and blessing we need to live for Him.

Adoration and a worshipful heart always lead to deeper repentance and create a selfless desire to give to God. In other words, worship begets worship.

CASTING DOWN THEIR GOLDEN CROWNS
Fifth, worship requires our self-renunciation before His glory. These elders around God's throne toss their crowns back at God's feet in an act of self-renunciation. Our God is a jealous God and will not share His glory with another!

And will cast their crowns before the throne.
(Revelation 4:10).

These crowns represent God's reward to the saints for faithful service accomplished in His name during their time on the earth. What a scene! All the believers in Heaven are tossing their crowns before God's throne! This act of worship visually reflects Paul's testimony, "By the grace of God I am what I am" (1 Corinthians 15:10). We compete in this life, like running a race, in order to win Heaven's ultimate prize—the incorruptible crown (9:24-25). And when we win God's reward at the end of life's race, we will realize even more fully that all we achieved for God in this world was accomplished by His grace and for His glory.

Think about it! He chose us, redeemed us, called us,

regenerated us, justified us, indwelt us, empowered us, planned good works for us to do, opened all the doors to make them happen, guided us, picked us up when we fell, forgave us, patiently waited on us, used us in spite of ourselves—and then crowned us!

Who do you think really deserves this crown?

Surely not us.

In humble recognition of this profound truth, we will cast our crowns back at His feet, symbols that "from Him and through Him and to Him are all things. To Him be the glory forever. Amen" (Romans 11:36).

What achievements and personal glory—even in this life—do you need to cast back at His feet?

Maybe someone has crowned you with a compliment for the great job you did serving God. Maybe someone has praised you for singing a solo. Or rewarded you for working in the church.

Just pass it on to the Lord. He is a jealous God who will not share His glory with another. Pass that compliment on to the Lord and say, "God, you and I both know it was all You!"

GIVE GOD THE GLORY!

Sixth, worship includes the exaltation of His name. The elders' worship gives glory to God by elevating God's name above every name. Here's what they say:

> *Worthy art Thou, our Lord and our God, to receive glory and honor and power; for Thou didst create all things, and because of Thy will they existed, and were created.*
> (Revelation 4:11)

These elders are chanting, "Worthy art Thou." That means He alone is worthy to be praised. They are saying that He is deserving of our worship. Just like "the laborer is worthy of his wages" (1 Timothy 5:18), so God, who is holy, sovereign, omnipotent, and immutable is uniquely qualified to be praised.

In John's day, this declaration was a clear contrast to the self-acclaimed deity of the Emperor Domitian. The Caesar's entrance in triumphant procession would be greeted with the words "Worthy art Thou"—while his devotees in the popular cult of emperor worship addressed him as "our Lord and our God." The Christians refused to confess the arrogant claims of Domitian. They would have no part in the idolatrous worship of a human ruler and many were tortured and killed!

Here God is revealing to these early believers—and to us today—that He alone is worthy to receive glory and honor and power.

No human is worthy. Only God is! Our greatest fulfillment is found in giving glory to God. In the words of the Shorter Catechism, "Man's chief end is to glorify God and to enjoy Him forever."

This praise is solidly based upon God's right as Creator—"For Thou didst create all things." Here's why praise should be given to God. Because He alone has the power to create all things out of nothing of His own purposes.

God declares, "It is I who made the earth, and created man upon it. I stretched out the heavens with My hands, and I ordained all their host" (Isaiah 45:12).

Why did God create? Simply because He chose to. Solely for His good pleasure. Here is a claim for His absolute sovereignty—a missing note in many churches today. God is His own reason. He is His own cause. God alone is the only cause and purpose for creation. We exist by His power, for His pleasure.

The world would rather choke than give such honor to God. For example, who do you think is behind the teaching of evolution? None other than Satan himself who attempts to steal glory from God as the Creator. In many classrooms God is blasphemed—stripped of His power to create, all in the name of scholarship. But in Heaven He is worshiped as Creator. Believe me, God suffers no identity crisis in Heaven!

LIFESTYLE WORSHIP

Do you see what the worship of Heaven involves? The angels and saints before God's throne worship Him with . . .

◆*A declaration of His greatness*
◆*A celebration of His goodness*
◆*A submission before His sovereignty*
◆*An adoration of His person*
◆*A self-renunciation before His glory*
◆*An exaltation of His name.*

That, my friend, is the true essence of genuine worship!

And this is the true essence of what it is to be heavenly minded. At the center of a mind set on things above is a heart that passionately worships God. The one who is heavenly minded is one who is a fervent worshiper.

Worship must be a way of life for us! Every moment of every day must be a worship service. As living sacrifices, we must consistently offer ourselves to God. Paul writes that such consecration is our spiritual service of worship (Romans 12:1).

May this heavenly scene be reproduced in our daily lives—time and time again. Here is who we must worship. Here is how we must worship.

Let's give Him the glory!

Chapter Four

I'VE JUST SEEN JESUS

The Lamb of Heaven

Revelation 5:1-7

A LOT OF PEOPLE THESE DAYS CLAIM TO HAVE gone to Heaven and seen Jesus. While flipping through a Christian magazine recently, I was overwhelmed with the advertisements of some religious leaders who say that when it comes to seeing Jesus in Heaven they've, well, *been there, done that.*

One such full-page spread invited people to attend an "I Walked in Heaven with Jesus" crusade. Now that's an attention getter! I was irresistibly lured to read on.

This one man in particular said, "Five-and-a-half days of glorious experiences inside of Heaven talking with the apostles, the prophets, the archangels, and hearing the voice of God recorded on twelve hours of tapes."

Of course, at the bottom of the page, there was the opportunity to "participate." An order form could be cut out and mailed in. It read, "Enclosed is my check or money order for sixty dollars."

What a steal—*literally!*

Another ad read, "I Saw Heaven." This proposition to get people to mail in their money pushed the envelope even further (no pun intended). It claimed that when this self-proclaimed guru was eight years old, "Jesus took him through Heaven and ordained him to the ministry. In the years since then, this remarkable young man has been faithful to his heavenly calling."

Now, that's a humble, *self*-written ad!

How are we to respond to such outlandish claims? Are

68

people really going to Heaven these days and seeing Jesus? Are they actually returning to earth with such amazing testimonies? Are these bizarre stories *true?*

I hate to be the bearer of bad news—but save your money.

Scripture clearly teaches such visions and experiences were restricted to the first-century apostles who formed the foundation of the Church (Ephesians 2:20, 3:5; 2 Corinthians 12:1-6).

Even the Apostle Paul was forbidden to talk about his heavenly vision because it might lead to boasting. Today such claims are at best the result of a man's creative imagination, not divine inspiration.

Who needs the childish perspective of an eight-year-old's trip to Heaven when we have what the mature Apostle John saw and recorded under the inspiration of the Holy Spirit in the book of Revelation? John's biblical account of his trip to Heaven pulls back the veil of eternity and allows us to view worlds unseen. In this account, John records for us his guided tour of Heaven and his vision of the glorified Christ. What John saw provides us with a heavenly perspective that we will not soon forget—a vision we desperately need today.

It had been sixty years since John last saw Christ face-to-face. On that occasion, Jesus ascended to Heaven from the Mount of Olives (Acts 1:9-11). Once before during our Lord's earthly ministry, John saw Jesus in His unveiled glory—on the Mount of Transfiguration (Matthew 17:1-2).

Now, in Heaven, John sees again the *glorified* Christ— *not* the humble Carpenter from Nazareth. John beholds Christ in His regal majesty. Exalted. Enthroned. Ruling. Reigning. King of kings. Lord of lords. What John records here is for our benefit that we, too, may behold Christ for who He is—the Sovereign Lord of all creation.

If we are to be heavenly minded, we must have this incredible vision of Christ at the very forefront of our thinking. It must be the filter through which we see and evaluate everything. The Bible says that our every thought must be taken captive to obedience to the glorified Christ—*every* thought! That's what it means to be heavenly minded.

Let's see the Christ John saw.

WHEN THE SCROLL IS CALLED UP YONDER

Immediately following the spontaneous worship of God in Heaven (Revelation 4:8-11), John now focuses upon an extraordinary sight.

> *I saw in the right hand of Him who sat on the throne a book written inside and on the back, sealed up with seven seals.* (Revelation 5:1)

In God's right hand—that place of greatest authority, highest privilege, and supreme importance—John sees a book. Actually, it's a long strip of paper or parchment rolled up like a scroll (*biblian*) and sealed shut so that it cannot be opened. This book is held tightly by God's omnipotent fist, indicating its divine source and that it is God's to give to whomever He pleases. This is uniquely *God's* book!

Oddly enough, this scroll is written on both sides— front and back. Ancients hardly ever wrote on both sides of a scroll. Usually only one side was for writing, while the back side was a rough, outer cover. Writing on both sides symbolized that the message was full to overflowing, detailed, and extremely important. The mere fact that it is written down as opposed to being spoken indicates that it is unalterable, settled, and determined by God alone.

In ancient times, a scroll—like a Roman will—was sealed by placing a single seal on the outer edge. But *this* scroll has seven seals, one on the outside and six more on the inside. In other words, the scroll was partially rolled and then sealed, rolled some more and then sealed, rolled again and then sealed, until the seventh seal sealed the entire scroll.

The fact that this scroll has seven seals means that it is locked up tighter than Fort Knox. It is inaccessible—a concealed mystery. It is a closed book, shut by seven seals, making it impossible for any man to open it, read it, and then execute its contents.

So what's in this scroll?

Countless possibilities have been offered. Some have suggested that this is the Lamb's book of life. Others say it is the book of redemption containing God's eternal plan of salvation. Still others believe it to be Christ's title deed to the earth. Or that it contains God's eternal decree.

Actually, this seal records God's predetermined decree for the consummation of this age. It contains the climactic events of world history immediately preceding the Second Coming of Christ. In this book are the final, end-time, cataclysmic judgments of God that will be poured out upon the earth during the great Tribulation. The One who possesses this book and can break its seals possesses the right to rule the world (Revelation 6:1,3,5,7,9,12; 8:1).

When this scroll is opened, the seven seal judgments (Revelation 6), the seven trumpet judgments (Revelation 8–9), and the seven bowl judgments (Revelation 16) are executed with severe wrath and universal judgment, ushering in the world Kingdom of Jesus Christ.

The prophet Ezekiel saw this scroll and wrote, "Then I looked, behold; a hand was extended to me; and lo, a scroll was in it. When he spread it out before me, it was written on the front and back; and written on it were lamentations, mourning and woe" (Ezekiel 2:9-10). It was a book that recorded the coming judgment of God upon the earth.

Likewise, Daniel the prophet saw the same scroll: "And there will be a time of distress such as never occurred since there was a nation until that time; and at that time your people, everyone who is found written in the book, will be rescued. . . . But as for you, Daniel, conceal these words and seal up the book until the end of time" (Daniel 12:1,4). The record of the unprecedented Tribulation and the events of the end of this age were recorded by Daniel in this book.

Lest we forget, this world is spinning through space, headed toward a final, cataclysmic judgment. Have we forgotten that the wrath of Christ is presently boiling over and one day will be unleashed on this ungodly world? In the end, Heaven will prove to be triumphant over the earth. This judgment during the Last Days is written by God in His sacred scroll, already divinely ordained and predestined to occur.

Here, in this scroll, is the final act of God's unfolding drama of redemptive history. John must have been overwhelmed with desire and anticipation at the thought of seeing a "sneak preview" of this world conquest and takeover.

CELESTIAL SEARCH COMMITTEE
With solemn tone, a mighty angel interrupts John's focus upon this mysterious scroll and asks an inescapable question.

> *I saw a strong angel proclaiming with a loud voice,*
> *"Who is worthy to open the book and to break its seals?"*
> *And no one in heaven, or on the earth, or under the*
> *earth, was able to open the book, or to look into it.*
> (Revelation 5:2-3)

This poignant question lies at the heart of the human dilemma. Who can rescue us from self-destruction and, worse, God's judgment? Who is capable of solving our problems? Who is wise enough to possess all the answers? Who is strong enough to pull it off? Who has the resources we need to solve our dilemma?

On a grand scale, this question asks, "Who is competent to bring human history to its appointed end? Who is qualified to overturn evil and make right all human injustices? Who is capable of ushering in peace and prosperity to the human scene? Who is fit to punish all wrong and reward right?"

So, a search is conducted throughout creation.

First, the executive search was conducted throughout Heaven. All Heaven was turned upside-down, but no created being was found worthy. No elect angel around the throne. No glorified saint in Heaven. No earthly ruler in glory. No one was found possessing the ability to open God's scroll and make it come to pass. *Not one!*

Then, a frantic search was made to the four corners of the earth. Every continent was investigated. But no one was found with the clout to break open the seals. The greatest world rulers of human history were all found to be incompetent. In John's day, Rome claimed to have all the answers. Caesar boasted of his imperial might. The Empire gloried in its genius. But a global search turned up not one qualified candidate. *Not one!*

Finally, a desperate search was made under the earth. The caverns of hell were explored. The pits of the inferno were ransacked. But no imprisoned demon, nor any damned soul was found who could do it. *Not one!*

All creation—Heaven, earth, and hell—was found to be absolutely, unequivocally incompetent to execute the events contained in the scroll (Revelation 6–22). All possibilities were exhausted and no one was found who could save the planet.

We are haunted with the same insurmountable dilemma today. Despite all the campaign promises and rhetoric of our politicians, no political party nor any government agency or social program is capable of ushering in a golden age of prosperity. Our problems are beyond us. No one in Washington has the answers. No one in Moscow. No one in London, Baghdad, Tel Aviv, or Tokyo can deliver us from our problems.

What an indictment! No one can execute God's plan for human history. We are hopeless and helpless to usher in the Golden Age. Let me say it again very clearly—our problems are beyond us.

TEARS IN HEAVEN

This futile search absolutely crushed John's heart! He dissolved emotionally. The future of the world seemed too bleak to face.

> *I began to weep greatly, because no one was found worthy to open the book, or to look into it.* (Revelation 5:4)

No wonder John wept! His troubled heart was filled with deep distress. Open lamentation. Heartrending sobs.

Deep grief. Loud wailing. Scalding tears. Unrestrained mourning. Unrestricted crying.

John was weeping because there was no relief in sight to man's distress. God's future Kingdom appears to be indefinitely postponed. God's final judgment seems to be canceled.

Absolutely no one was found who could save mankind from its problems. No one who could solve the haunting issues that threaten us. No one who could restrain the forces of evil. No one who could defend the helpless. No one who could protect the innocent.

Could it be that this scroll would not be opened? Would the conclusion to God's redemptive history be forever suspended?

As I write this chapter, I am watching another election return—and now, more than ever, I feel John's hopeless despair. Even our best politicians promise us so much. But they hold out such puny solutions to our mounting problems. Quite frankly, it's enough to make a grown man cry. Which is exactly what John did.

John's tears represent the weeping of all God's people down through the centuries. These are the tears of Adam and Eve driven from the Garden. These are the tears of ancient Israel in Egyptian bondage. These are the tears of the early Church longing for relief from the Roman Empire. These are our tears longing for God to make a disordered world right.

THE LION KING!
Suddenly, John is given an insight that hits him like a ton of bricks.

> *One of the elders said to me, "Stop weeping; behold the Lion that is from the tribe of Judah, the root of David, has overcome so as to open the book and its seven seals."* (Revelation 5:5)

One of the elders around God's throne interrupts John's weeping, bringing a needed word of rebuke and comfort.

This messenger sees beyond John's limited human perspective to God's eternal solution.

The elder forbids John to weep any longer—"Stop weeping!" Crying was totally inappropriate and out of place.

Instead, this saint redirects John's attention to the only solution that exists to the human dilemma—but there *is* a solution! "Behold, the Lion," he says, "that is from the tribe of Judah."

The tribe of Judah was the tribe of David from which the kingly line proceeded (Genesis 49:9-10). It was to this tribe that the promise was given of a Son whose throne and kingdom would endure forever (2 Samuel 7:13,16). He would be named Immanuel—God with us (Isaiah 7:14)! The Messiah would come through the lineage of David as a greater son of David (Luke 1:32-33). Like a lion—ferocious, bold, courageous, fearless, strong, aggressive, kingly, mighty, majestic.

This Lion of Judah is *Jesus Christ!* He alone is able to break the seals, open the scroll, and execute its events.

Likewise, the elder says that this Lion-King is the Root of David. He who came *after* David as the offspring of David, but was also *before* him as the root (Revelation 22:16). This points to Jesus' eternal preexistence. Jesus was a descendent of David as "the Root of David."

This regal Lion—eternal, divine, yet completely human—overcame so as to open the scroll. Jesus conquered sin in order to implement what is written in the scroll. He won the victory at the cross in order to open this scroll.

THE LAMB WHO ROARS

Eagerly John turns his head to see the Lion. But the apostle is not prepared for what he sees. Expecting to see a kingly Lion, the apostle sees something totally different.

> *I saw between the throne (with the four living creatures) and the elders a Lamb standing, as if slain, having seven horns and seven eyes, which are the seven Spirits of God, sent out into all the earth.* (Revelation 5:6)

When John turns to look, he doesn't see a Lion. Instead, he sees . . . what? A Lamb! Straining to see a ferocious lion, John sees an innocent, seemingly defenseless lamb. John must have wondered, *"This is the solution to the world's problems? A lowly lamb? A weak, submissive sheep?"* Precisely. The answer to man's problems is the Lamb of God—Jesus Christ. The Lion-Lamb. The Sovereign Savior. What a combination of meekness and majesty!

A lamb pictures Christ in His humble submission and obedient sacrifice. This is a staggering picture of Christ, the Lion-Lamb, who conquered through submission. He triumphed through obedience!

This Lamb is in the center of all Heaven, immediately between—or in the midst of, more correctly—the heavenly throne. He occupies the throne of God in that place of sole preeminence (Revelation 3:21). He is the centerpiece of all the angelic host and redeemed saints.

In describing this Lamb, John describes four essential truths about Christ. John sees Him as slain yet standing sovereignly with searching gaze.

Scarred, but Not Beyond Recognition!

First, *this Lamb is slain*. John sees "the Lamb . . . as if slain" (Revelation 5:6). The word for *slain (sphazo)*, means to cut up and mutilate an animal sacrifice. It speaks of a violent, bloody slaughter. It describes the gory crucifixion of our Lord Jesus Christ. Thorns pierced his skull. A whip lacerated His back. Fists bruised His face. Nails gouged His hands. A spear tore His side. Blood and water came gushing out.

As the Lamb of God, Jesus bore our sins and absorbed the full wrath of God as He hung suspended upon the cross (1 Peter 2:24, 3:18). He was crushed, smitten, afflicted, pierced through, scourged, chastened, and oppressed for our iniquities, cut off from the land of the living, according to Isaiah 53:4-6. Now, in Heaven, Jesus still bears the marks of His death in His resurrected body. Nail-pierced hands and a spear-torn side still scar and disfigure His glorified body as eternal visual reminders of His death for our sins.

Sixty years earlier, John, along with the other disciples,

was in the upper room one week after Christ's resurrection. Seven days earlier, Thomas was so discouraged that he doubted the disciples' report that Jesus had triumphed over death.

Suddenly the risen Christ appeared to the disciples. And Jesus said to Thomas, "Reach here your finger, and see My hands; and reach here your hand, and put it into My side" (John 20:27). When Thomas saw the tangible marks of death in Christ's resurrection body, he confessed, "My Lord and my God!"

A Sunday school teacher of young boys once asked her class, "Is there anything manmade in Heaven?"

To her surprise, one of the young boys spoke up and said, "Yes, Ma'am, there is."

"What could there possibly be in Heaven that is man-made?" she asked.

"The nail prints in Jesus' hands," the little boy answered.

What Thomas saw in the upper room, and what John looked upon in Heaven, must grip our lives as well. Let us forever consider these visual reminders of His crucifixion and wonder that such amazing love should be shown to undeserving sinners like you and me.

Standing Room Only

Second, *this Lamb is standing.* John writes, "I saw . . . the Lamb standing" (Revelation 5:6). John looks more closely and discovers something even more strange. This slain Lamb, who was violently slaughtered and put to death, is actually standing! Having been killed, He is now alive *again!* The Bible says that God put His own Son to death, but then brought Him back to life (Romans 4:24). God the Father raised Christ from the grave of defeat, forever to be victorious over death.

This truth dominated the preaching of the early church. On the day of Pentecost, Peter declared,

> *This Man, delivered up by the predetermined plan and*
> *foreknowledge of God, you nailed to a cross by the hands*

*of godless men and put Him to death. And God raised
Him up again, putting an end to the agony of death,
since it was impossible for Him to be held in its power.*
(Acts 2:23-24)

At Calvary, it appeared—from the human perspective—that evil had triumphed over good. The God-Man
was put to death by the cruelest means of torture ever
devised by wicked men—a Roman execution called
crucifixion. Jesus died with all the vestures of defeat. A cross.
Three nails. A crown of thorns. A jeering mob. A black sky.
An agonizing cry. Unquestionably, this was the blackest
hour in human history.

But then came Sunday morning, and with it the glorious report, "He is risen!" Evil's triumph was short-lived.
Death was swallowed up. The grave defanged. The resurrection of God's Lamb, Jesus Christ, opened up the gates of
Paradise for all who would put their personal trust in Him!

The originator of a new religion came to the great
French diplomat-statesman, Charles Maurice de Talleyrand-
Perigord and complained that he could not make any
converts.

"What should I do?" he asked.

"I should recommend," said Talleyrand, "that you get
yourself crucified and then die, but be sure to rise again on
the third day."

Jesus Christ *was* raised from the dead and He will be surrounded by His converts throughout eternity.

Horns of Plenty

Third, *the Lamb is sovereign.* John sees "the Lamb . . . having
seven horns" (Revelation 5:6) indicating His absolute, unrivaled strength over all. In Scripture, an animal's horns speak
of its power to ram, butt, gore, and defeat its enemies, and
seven is the number of fullness. Seven horns means
omnipotence. As God's Lamb with seven horns, the risen
Christ now commands the nations, controls the universe,
and dictates the destinies of all creation with unrivaled
power over the kings of the earth.

Paul boasts, "He [Christ] . . . is the blessed and only Sovereign, the King of kings, and Lord of lords" (1 Timothy 6:15). Likewise, he writes, "[God] seated Him at His right hand in the heavenly places, far above all rule and authority and power and dominion, and every name that is named, not only in this age, but also in the one to come. And He put all things under His feet" (Ephesians 1:20-22).

Jesus reigns supreme over all creation—over Heaven, earth, and hell. He rules over the visible world, as well as the invisible spiritual world. In Him, all things hold together. He is the omnipotent God who keeps all the planets in space in motion. He is the energy of the universe who keeps all things in their place. He is the preeminent One, highest in rank, the rightful heir of all creation (Colossians 1:15-18).

The Lamb is sovereign!

The "Eyes" Have It

Fourth, *this Lamb is searching.* John sees "the Lamb . . . having seven eyes" (Revelation 5:6). In Scripture, eyes speak of intelligence, wisdom, discernment, and understanding. The number seven indicates the Lamb's perfect and full understanding of all human history and every individual life. With seven eyes, He looks over all the earth.

God's Lamb is omniscient. Full of intelligence. Possessing perfect discernment. Given inscrutable understanding. He has perfect knowledge of all things past, present, and future. He operates His Kingdom not according to mere rumors or hearsay, but by truth and reality.

This is one Lamb who can't have the wool pulled over His eyes! Isaiah wrote of His searching, unfathomable omniscience,

> *The Spirit of the LORD will rest on Him, the Spirit of wisdom and understanding, the spirit of counsel and strength, the spirit of knowledge and the fear of the LORD. . . . He will not judge by what His eyes see, nor make a decision by what His ears hear; but with righteousness He will judge the poor, and decide with fairness for the afflicted of the earth.* (Isaiah 11:2-4)

TAKING THE REIGNS

Now, in one dramatic moment, Jesus Christ, the Lion-Lamb, boldly approaches the throne of God. He approaches the Father and takes the scroll from the right hand of the Father. What no one else could do, Jesus Christ now does. No man nor angel could take the scroll—but Christ takes it to be His own. He alone can break open its seals. He alone can execute its judgments.

> *And He came, and He took it out of the right hand of Him who sat on the throne.* (Revelation 5:7)

In this one momentous act, Jesus Christ secures the seven-sealed scroll from the Father's right hand. Before the watching eyes of all Heaven, Christ decisively claims the right to rule.

The search is now complete. Our Sovereign Lord assumes the absolute authority to bring all human history to its appointed end. This dramatic "takeover" reveals that the Lion has taken the bull by the horns. Christ, vested with divine authority, is now poised and ready to conquer all God's enemies. He alone can judge the world, both the living and the dead, and execute the final judgments upon the earth.

Here is one of the most graphic pictures of Christ's lordship recorded anywhere in Scripture—dramatic, awesome, and emotionally charged. Here is Christ taking the divine scroll and, with it, the right to bring history to its appointed end. Jesus Christ now receives from the Father His inheritance as the rightful Heir of Heaven and earth.

What this says is that behind the scenes of history—in the unseen world of Heaven—Jesus Christ is enthroned and reigning supremely as Lord over all! We are not creatures abandoned on a planet spinning madly through space, lost in the vast galaxies. Rather, the Lion-Lamb now sits in power, executing His eternal decrees for all human history.

No matter how dominant the forces of evil may appear to be today, they are powerless to annul even one word of what is written in God's sovereign scroll.

What a vision!
Hallelujah! What a Savior!

HEAVEN ON EARTH

What John saw so long ago in Heaven, must be our vision every moment of every day. We must see everything through the grid of the lordship of Jesus Christ. To be worldly minded is to live for the things of this world. But to be heavenly minded is to live for Him who reigns above.

Christ is the centerpiece of Heaven. All Heaven revolves around Him. Similarly, the one who is heavenly minded lives with Christ as the centerpiece of his life. Everything in our lives must revolve around Him!

In what areas of your life does Christ need to be central? Where has He lost preeminence in your life? Your thought life? Your business? Your service? Your marriage?

Why not take a moment right now before you turn this page and allow Christ to assume His rightful place in your life—the place of preeminence, the place of authority, the place of lordship. Allow Him to rule and reign in your life. Make Christ the focus. Crown Him Lord of all.

Do it *now!*

Chapter Five

Singing in the Reign

The Worship of Heaven
(Part Two)

Revelation 5:8-14

SEVENTY-THOUSAND PLUS WERE JAM-PACKED INTO the Cotton Bowl that hot summer night in Texas. But this time, it wasn't for just another football game. This evening would be *far more* important.

The Vietnam War had just ended and billionaire businessman H. Ross Perot had personally rented this historic stadium to pay tribute to our returning soldiers. In typical Perot fashion, this Texas tycoon paid to bring to Dallas any soldier who had fought in the steamy jungles and rice fields of Nam who wanted to be present.

It was a night to remember!

On one goal line, a large platform was built for "America's entertainer," Bob Hope, and the other celebrities who had gathered for the welcome home party. As the gala evening began, the stadium was packed and the celebrities were ready, but the field was completely empty. Rows of vacant chairs lined the gridiron.

Suddenly, the military band struck up "Stars and Stripes Forever" and music filled the Texas night air. A solitary American flag was dramatically hoisted atop the stadium, which brought tears to the eyes of even the bravest men present. Then, a procession of American soldiers began marching out the end zone tunnel, streaming down the ramp and pouring onto the field.

As these valiant warriors—true American heroes— came out, the entire stadium spontaneously rose to its feet. Clapping. Cheering. Whistling. Yelling. Hollering. Jabbing fists into the air. Waving American flags overhead. The ovation was *deafening!*

I know because I was there. I've been in the Cotton Bowl for many historic sporting events—Cotton Bowl classics, Dallas Cowboy games, Oklahoma—Texas clashes, and Southwest Conference skirmishes. But never have I heard the cheering as loud as it was that night. As the stream of soldiers kept pouring onto the playing field—and as their numbers grew larger and larger—the crowd's ovation grew louder and louder.

Then came an *unforgettable* sight.

At the end of this triumphant procession came those brave men who had been seriously injured during the Vietnam War. Maimed and crippled, these returning heroes paraded onto the field of the Cotton Bowl. But their march was much slower.

Some came limping out on crutches. Some staggered out with canes. Others hobbled out without a leg. Still others walked out with heads bandaged, attended by nurses. Then came blind soldiers, men who had lost their eyesight in the war, led by the arm of a fellow soldier.

In a most dramatic fashion, which I will never forget, there came an entourage of soldiers who were pushed onto the football field in *wheelchairs*. These men, unable to even walk, were escorted to the fifty-yard line, bringing to completion this victory procession.

By this time, the emotionally charged crowd was all but standing on their seats, cheering their heroes home. The roar was deafening! It was a privilege just to be in the presence of such valiant men.

It was these last soldiers—these men who paid the greatest price—who were the *true heroes* of the war. They shed their life's blood for the cause of freedom and many suffered the loss of limbs. Their injuries were the most severe. Their service, the greatest. Their loss, the deepest. As it should be, they were the most deserving of the loudest ovation. Their *greater* sacrifice made them the *most* worthy of ovation.

THE APPLAUSE OF HEAVEN

That scene in the Cotton Bowl years ago foreshadows a scene that will be duplicated, again and again, throughout the ages to come in Heaven. God's Lamb—Jesus Christ—gave His life at the Cross for us. He was brutally slain and He violently died for our sins. He paid the greatest price. His pain was the deepest. His suffering, the greatest. Therefore, He is, unquestionably, *most* deserving to be worshiped.

One day, we will find ourselves in Heaven's grandstands, surrounding God's throne (Hebrews 12:1). We will behold Jesus Christ—the Lamb slain, standing—in full, unveiled glory. We will respond with heartfelt worship as we have never adored Him before. The applause of Heaven will grow louder as we grow exponentially in our understanding of His worthiness.

Christ will bear visual reminders in His body of His costly victory won at the cross. We will see His nail-pierced hands and spear-thrust side, and we will shout for joy. We will see Him standing in glory, seated at the right hand of God the Father and praise Him forever and ever. Our worship in Heaven will be so *fervent* in that day!

If we are to worship Christ today, even in small measure the way we will worship Him then, we must have this vision of Christ. We must set our minds on things above where Christ is seated at God's right hand (Colossians 3:1-3). We must see Christ as He is *now* in glory, and only then will our hearts overflow in true worship as we were designed to do.

What we have in Revelation 5 is a vision of Christ (verses 1-7) and the expanding, concentric circles of His worshipers in Heaven. First, we see the worship of Jesus Christ in Heaven by those immediately around the throne (verses 8-10); then we see worship throughout all Heaven (verses 11-12); finally we see worship throughout all the universe (verses 13-14). Beginning with those angels and saints immediately before God's throne and then expanding outward to the furthest realms of darkness, we witness the proper worship due our Sovereign Lord.

Here is worship as it was meant to be—alive, dynamic, genuine, blazing, passionate.

FLAT ON THEIR FACES

Heaven's worship begins with those in closest proximity to God's throne—the cherubim and elders—and then, like a "wave" at a football game, it spreads to all creation. But first the worship begins with those closest to the throne. John writes:

> *And when He had taken the book, the four living creatures and the twenty-four elders fell down before the Lamb.* (Revelation 5:8)

As you recall from the last chapter, God held the seven-sealed scroll in His right hand, which contains the final act of redemptive history. A search of the entire universe found no one worthy to open the scroll and execute its contents. John began to weep that the scroll would be forever sealed—never to be executed. With a godly jealousy for God's Kingdom to triumph, the seer wept.

John's disappointment lifted when an unidentified angel pointed to Him who alone is worthy to take the scroll and break its seals. That One was Jesus Christ! He took the scroll out of God's right hand and the momentous transfer of the scroll from God's hand to Jesus Christ creates an overwhelming response in Heaven. A spontaneous explosion of praise erupts around God's throne.

All Heaven breaks loose!

The four living creatures—angelic attendants around the throne—fall down on their faces and begin to worship the Lord Jesus Christ. Then the twenty-four elders—representing the redeemed of all the ages—join in with them in worshiping the Lamb.

All Heaven—angels and saints alike—fall down like cut timber before God in utter humility and submission. They are overawed by the glory of the Lion King, the Lord Jesus Christ. They are knocked flat on their faces by His regal splendor. This shouldn't surprise us because any time someone is in God's presence, whether on earth or in Heaven, they *always* react this way. Why? They've seen the glory of God, that's why!

John MacArthur tells about meeting a man who claims that he was shaving one morning when Jesus Christ appeared to him. "Do you believe me?" the man asked MacArthur.

"Did you keep shaving?" MacArthur asked him.

"Yes."

"Then it wasn't Jesus," MacArthur responded. "If it had been Jesus, you would have fallen on your face before Him."

People in the presence of the glorified Christ *always* fall down before Him. If the back doors of the sanctuary were to swing open suddenly and the glorified Christ Himself were to walk down the center aisle during one of our Sunday worship services, the entire congregation would immediately fall on its face before Him. Every knee would bow before Him. There would be no dancing in the aisles. No immediate round of applause. Instead, God's people would prostrate themselves before Him.

I remember being in a special meeting of civic leaders in downtown Little Rock, Arkansas. The special occasion was the upcoming Billy Graham Crusade. Seated at the head table were all the leading dignitaries of our city and state. I was seated at a table next to the inside aisle.

Midway through the program, the emcee on the front platform was speaking when I suddenly sensed someone walking right past me through the crowd.

As I turned to see who it was, I heard hundreds of chairs being pushed back. The entire room rose simultaneously to its feet.

It was Billy Graham! His plane had just landed and he was quickly escorted into this meeting already in progress. Unannounced, Mr. Graham was led to the head table.

Even the head speaker stopped talking. Everyone in the room stood to their feet. Every eye was riveted upon him. Everyone clapped for this man of God, then cheered. The ovation grew louder and louder until Billy reached the platform.

In Heaven, the effect will be much the same yet, at the same time, greatly different. Instead of rising to our feet, we will all fall flat on our faces before the living Christ. And give Him the glory!

Such humble submission should mark our worship today. No one may come proudly strutting into God's presence. Only those who lower themselves before Him may worship. "God is opposed to the proud, but gives grace to the humble" (1 Peter 5:5). I fear that, in the midst of our entertainment-crazed society, there's too much flesh on parade in the average worship service, and too little self-abasing humility.

HARPS ARE INSTRUMENTAL

As all Heaven collapses before the throne, each celestial cherubim (the four living creatures) holds in his hand a musical instrument—a harp.

> *Having each one a harp, and golden bowls full of incense, which are the prayers of the saints.* (Revelation 5:8)

Throughout the Bible, the harp is an instrument of joy and gladness. In fact, the harp is used in Scripture more than any other instrument to praise God. The psalmist wrote, "I will . . . praise Thee with a harp" (Psalm 71:22).

There are, I believe, many other musical instruments in Heaven with which to worship God. Here on earth, the Bible says, every instrument should be used to praise God. The same must be true in Heaven.

> *Praise Him with trumpet sound;*
> *Praise Him with harp and lyre.*
> *Praise Him with timbrel and dancing;*
> *Praise Him with stringed instruments and pipe.*
> *Praise Him with loud cymbals;*
> *Praise Him with resounding cymbals.*
> *Let everything that has breath praise the* LORD.
> *Praise the Lord!* (Psalm 150:3-6)

Every musical instrument known to man can be employed to offer praise to God—from a grand piano to a washboard. No instrument should remain silent. All should be used for its highest purpose—to glorify God.

One day, Heaven's orchestra will blow us away when it strikes up its praise for God. Trumpets. Harps. Lyres. Timbrels. Instruments. Pipes. Loud cymbals. All the instruments peeling the paint off the walls of the throne room.

Some dour believers, when they get to Heaven, are going to be surprised, if not shocked, at the plethora of musical instruments used in Heaven's worship—instruments far beyond those used in eighteenth-century England.

HEAVEN SCENT

Likewise, each saint holds a golden bowl of incense. Such a bowl was a container with a large, open mouth, used for offering incense at the altar in the tabernacle and temple.

Symbolically, these bowls contain the prayers of the saints in Heaven. Do believers pray in Heaven? What are saints doing praying in Heaven?

These prayers are the pleadings of saints already in Heaven, requesting that God make right every wrong on the earth. These prayers are petitions offered to God to vindicate His name on the earth by pouring out His judgments upon an unbelieving world.

Remember, saints in Heaven are glorified; thus, they are perfected in the image of Christ. We will be without any sin. Therefore, these prayers are *perfect* petitions offered from *perfected* people in a *perfect* place—Heaven. What they pray is *right!* These saints are asking God to do that which perfectly conforms with His holy character—that is, judge sin on the earth. Be assured, these prayers *will* be answered. God will punish every wrong in due time.

SONG SUNG NEW

The inner chambers of Heaven are filled with resounding anthems of praise sung to God. Holy angels and redeemed saints alike are singing with glorified voices to God.

And they sang a new song, saying, "Worthy art Thou to take the book, and to break its seals; for Thou wast slain, and didst purchase for God with Thy blood men from every tribe and tongue and people and nation. And Thou hast made them to be a kingdom and priests to our God; and they will reign upon the earth." (Revelation 5:9-10)

There will be new songs to sing in Heaven, new songs to express our new love for God. Why a new song? Because the old songs just won't do. A vastly increased awareness of His glory will compel us to express deeper gratitude and higher praise. Only a new song of praise, inspired by a new awareness of His mercies, will suffice.

This isn't the first new song God has given believers. When we first trusted Christ to be our Lord and Savior, God put a new song in our mouths (Psalm 33:3, 40:3). New joy was ours because the burden of sin was lifted. Now, once more, God will give us a new song. Again, a new joy will be ours when, in Heaven, we express our new heartfelt devotion for Christ.

Men and women from every continent and every age will join in this worship. From every conceivable background, men and women in Heaven will worship Christ. Every descent. Every clan. Every family lineage. Every age. Every language group. Every race. Every nation. Every political party. All groups will praise God.

Listen to the new song they are singing in Heaven. Everyone is singing this song—angels and redeemed saints alike. All the voices of Heaven are joining together to form one mighty choir. Think of the sheer volume of this anthem of praise!

This heavenly hymn begins by declaring that Jesus Christ alone is the One worthy to take God's book and break open its seals. He alone is capable and qualified. Only Christ can bring human history to its appointed end. He alone can judge the earth and usher in God's Kingdom.

The song looks back to Christ's bloodstained cross and exalts His once-for-all finished work at Calvary. There, while hanging upon that cross, He bore our sins and purchased us with His blood. Throughout all eternity, we will praise Jesus Christ for His great victory won for us at the cross.

91

JESUS PAID IT ALL

The word *purchase* pictures the acquisition of slaves in a marketplace and then setting them free. That's what Christ did for us at the cross. He came into this world and—with the gold of His blood and silver of His tears—paid the purchase price for a lost humanity who had become enslaved to sin. Only Jesus can set us free (John 8:36).

All the religions of the world can be put into one of two categories. On one side, there's the religion of human achievement. On the other, there's the religion of divine accomplishment. All religions, except one, teach that man must do good works and earn his way to Heaven. Only Christianity teaches that salvation is a free gift offered to undeserving sinners on the basis of the finished work of Christ at the cross. Only faith in Christ saves.

That's why in Heaven we will be praising Christ. We will not be praising ourselves, because no amount of good works, church membership, baptismal certificates, or service can take away sin. Only Christ can save us from sin.

Christ's victorious death at the cross—a death that brought about the death of death for all humankind—won the victory for men and women out of every part of the human race. He purchased a people for God from every conceivable background, without distinction of ethnic race, geographical location, or political persuasion. *Tribe* means the same descent, same clan, same family lineage. *Tongue* means people speaking the same language. *People* means those of the same race. *Nation* refers to those bound together by political unity, habits, and customs. People of every lineage, language, race, and political orientation will be in Heaven praising Christ.

Let me be clear: This heavenly hymn does not teach universalism. Every person will not be ultimately saved and find his or her way to Heaven. But people *out of* every people group will be there. How will people from groups that never heard the gospel be in Heaven?

Two factors come to bear upon this question. First, Jesus said that the gospel will be preached to all the world by the end of the age (Matthew 24:14). This includes all people groups who will be eventually reached for Christ. Second, I believe that those who die an early death—babies, infants, fetuses aborted—go into the presence of God. Every people group experiences these untimely tragedies and, thus, populates Heaven.

All who receive Jesus Christ by faith are made "a kingdom and priests to God." We are given all the rights of heavenly citizenship as subjects in the Kingdom of God. Likewise, we are made priests with full and immediate access into God's presence. What privilege is ours! One day we will serve God as reigning powers, the equivalents of kings, and share in Christ's rule in the Kingdom to come.

Paul said, "Do you not know that we shall judge angels?" (1 Corinthians 6:3).

GOD LIKES IT LOUD!

The company of worshipers expands and enlarges to include all the angels in Heaven. A second choir of worshipers joins now with the first choir. All Heaven breaks loose!

> *I looked, and I heard the voice of many angels around the throne and the living creatures and the elders; and the number of them was myriads of myriads, and thousands of thousands, saying with a loud voice. . . .* (Revelation 5:11)

Joining now with the cherubim—those angels nearest the throne—and with glorified believers are all the angelic host. How many angels is that? John says "myriads of myriads." So, again, how many is that? There simply wasn't a higher number in the Greek language that could be used. *Myriad (miros)* means ten thousand. Myriad of myriad means ten thousand times ten thousand—that's one hundred million! But this is in the plural—myriads of myriads—meaning hundreds of millions times hundreds of millions. The number is easily in the billions. That is an *extremely* high number. Multiplied billions are in this heavenly choir worshiping God in Heaven!

Then John records that there are still "thousands of thousands" in addition to the billions. One thousand times one thousand is one million. But, again, this is in the plural. So, there are multiplied millions spilling over the billions of worshipers already counted. This staggering number exceeds the limits of human language and our ability to comprehend. Here is a *countless* number of angels lifting their voices to God in praise.

Daniel, who was also privileged to be given a direct vision of Heaven, had the same problem counting this inestimable crowd of angels. The prophet wrote, "His [God's] vesture was like white snow, and the hair of His head like pure wool. His throne was ablaze with flames. Its wheels were a burning fire. A river of fire was flowing and coming out from before Him; *thousands upon thousands* were attending Him; and *myriads upon myriads* were standing before Him" (Daniel 7:9-10).

The psalmist declared, "The chariots of God are *myriads, thousands upon thousands*" (Psalm 68:17).

These multiplied billions and countless millions of angels are all singing with "loud voices." In the original Greek language, the manuscripts read *phone megale,* or literally, "with megaphones." This chant of celebration is a deafening roar! So loud that even those saints over seventy years old can hear! This is no hushed, quiet worship service. This is an *explosion* of celebration!

The heavenly chorus sings that the Lamb is worthy to receive praise. As the Lamb slain for sinners, His humble obedience at the cross uniquely qualifies Him to be worshiped.

On a much smaller scale, I have experienced something like this scene. Several times it has been my privilege to sit on the platform at a Billy Graham Crusade and hear the anthems of praise sung by over fifty thousand people. I can never hear such loud singing expressing adoration of Christ without beginning to weep. What must await us in Heaven?

MARY'S LITTLE LAMB
Jesus Christ is now receiving the fullness of His rightful inheritance. Worshipers in Heaven respond by lifting up the name of Christ. They declare that He is worthy to receive

the scroll and, along with it, power, riches, wisdom, might, honor, glory, and blessing. The first four He receives from God taking the scroll. The last three come from the worshipers of Heaven.

Worthy is the Lamb that was slain to receive power and riches and wisdom and might and honor and glory and blessing. (Revelation 5:12)

In taking the divine scroll, He is receiving the right to bring history to its appointed end. With that right come the qualifications necessary to accomplish that consummation. Those qualifications are power, riches, wisdom, and might.

First, the worshipers recognized the appropriateness of Christ receiving power. Power *(dunamis)* means His sheer control over all the created order. When the scroll of the Tribulation is opened, the world will see Christ's power to harness the wind, cause earthquakes, send famines and plagues, transform water into blood, and raise the dead (see Revelation 6–19).

Second, Jesus is worthy to receive *riches.* In taking the scroll, Jesus also receives riches. Riches means spiritual and material wealth. All of the resources, spiritual and material, of Heaven and earth are at His disposal to use in accomplishing His divine agenda.

Third, Jesus is worthy to receive wisdom. The word *(sophia)* means the ability to choose the best plans to accomplish the highest goals. This refers to Christ's ability to employ His limitless power and spend His inexhaustible riches to fulfill God's appointed program.

Fourth, Jesus receives might. Here is additional strength beyond His infinite power already mentioned. He has unlimited, infinite strength to defeat all our enemies and will use it during end-time events.

The next three—honor, glory, and blessing—refer to different aspects of the worship the Sovereign Lamb is worthy to receive.

Fifth, Jesus is worthy to receive *honor.* Honor *(timen)* refers to the reverence and adoration due Him as our sovereign Lord. "God highly exalted Him, and bestowed on Him the name which is above every name" (Philippians 2:9).

Sixth, they acknowledge that Jesus is worthy of *glory.* He is to be greatly praised because of His intrinsic deity, heavenly radiance, and holy majesty. He is worthy of our worship because He alone bridged the gap for us between Heaven and hell. We must give Him the praise that is due His name. What better place to give Him glory than with multiplied billions of saints and angels in the eternal home He's made possible for us?

Finally, Jesus is worthy to receive blessing. The word (*eulogian*) means that Christ is worthy of our speaking favorable things about Him and our declaring His excellencies. At funerals, the deceased is eulogized. People stand up and speak well of him. They mention specific virtues and accomplishments. These inhabitants of Heaven remind us of eulogizing not the dead but the living—the risen, reigning Christ.

Do you not see here that worship is no mindless, emotional babbling, but the passionate reciting of God's character and attributes back to Him? Worship is the natural response of our hearts when we behold the greatness of God.

ALL HAIL THE POWER!

Even all the worship of Heaven above is not enough. Jesus is so great, He deserves even greater praise. Now the company of worshipers in John's vision expands exponentially to encompass all creation. Everything. Everyone. Everywhere. All that God created will one day give Him glory. Finally, John records:

> *And every created thing which is in heaven and on the earth and under the earth and on the sea, and all things in them, I heard saying, "To Him who sits on the throne, and to the Lamb, be blessing and honor and glory and dominion forever and ever."* (Revelation 5:13)

Who comprises this outermost circle of worshipers? All those in Heaven, earth, and hell. All those in Heaven refers to the countless host of cherubim, seraphim, angelic beings, and redeemed saints. All those on the earth are living saints, unbelievers, Satan, and loosed demons. All those under the earth are all imprisoned demons and damned souls in hell. In other words, all intelligent life created by God will one day do that for which they were originally created—worship God.

This scene is anticipatory of that great final day when "every knee should bow, of those who are in heaven, and on earth, and under the earth, and that every tongue should confess that Jesus Christ is Lord, to the glory of God the Father" (Philippians 2:10-11).

Every knee will bow—every tongue will confess—every created being will one day declare that Jesus is Lord!

There will be no atheists in that day. There will be multitudes of lost theists, but no atheists. No one will deny the existence of God when they stand before Him. Even every unbeliever will fully acknowledge that Jesus Christ is Lord.

The atheist will realize what a grave mistake he made in his choice to worship counterfeit gods, whether that be nature, idols, other gods, material things, or himself. Suddenly, unalterably, eternally, all creation will confess Christ's lordship—but it will be too late. Nevertheless, they will say—as their own profession condemns them—"Jesus Christ is Lord."

"As I live, says the Lord, every knee shall bow to Me, and every tongue shall give praise to God" (Romans 14:11). Everything that has life and breath will praise Him—angels and demons, saved and lost humanity.

That reminds me of a T-shirt I saw. Printed on the front was, "God is dead."—Nietzsche.

But on the back, it said, "Nietzsche is dead."—God.

Yes, God will have the final word.

When he returned from traveling in space, Gherman Titov, the Russian cosmonaut, boasted, "Some people say there is a God out there . . . but in my travels around the earth . . . I saw no God or angels. I don't believe in God. I believe in man."

What a pity! All Titov had to do was to step out of his

spaceship without any life support. Then he would have met the one true, living God—in a heartbeat!

These worshipers declare that the Son is worthy to be given blessing, honor, glory, and dominion. Forever and ever. Infinitely. Indefinitely. Eternally. If ever there was a clear statement of Christ's deity, this is it. The same worship given to God is given to Christ. Clearly, Jesus is God and must be worshiped as God.

THE ELDERS' LAST STAND

Finally, to complete the scene, John records:

> *And the four living creatures kept saying, "Amen." And the elders fell down and worshiped.* (Revelation 5:14)

It's not that the angels praise God just once and that's it. They keep on worshiping Him—over and over. They never tire of giving Him glory. After each of His divine attributes is praised, there is a corresponding "Amen" shouted back loudly in response.

One side of Heaven yells out, "Blessing," and the other half yells back "Amen!" One half shouts "Honor," then the others affirm "Amen." The elders say "Glory" and the cherubim respond "Amen." The elders say "Dominion" and the angels echo "Amen." All this worship volleys back and forth in Heaven, ringing throughout the halls of glory.

At Arkansas Razorback football games, fifty thousand fans pack into War Memorial Stadium to witness the spectacle. The atmosphere is electric. One of the more exciting moments is when one-half of the stadium yells, "Arkansas!" and the other half of the stadium responds, "Razorbacks!" This cheer rallies back and forth, back and forth, building louder and louder.

"Arkansas!"

"Razorbacks!"

"Arkansas!"

"Razorbacks!"

Perhaps that's the way it will be in Heaven.

"Blessing!"

"Amen!"

"Honor!"
"Amen!"
"Glory!"
"Amen!"

This scene now ends the way it began. It has come full circle with the elders flat on their faces before God in humble worship. They prostrate themselves in worship before Him, acknowledging His greatness and glory. This tells us how we ought to begin and conclude each day—on our faces before God in humble worship.

When I graduated from Dallas Theological Seminary, I participated in a scene something like this. At graduation exercises, the graduating senior class traditionally sings the first verse of the school's official song—"All Hail the Power of Jesus' Name," (sung to the Diadem setting). I knew that I had graduated when I sung together with my classmates this glorious hymn. Tears flowed from my eyes. Goose bumps stood on my arms. My voice quivered with deep emotion.

But then, for the final verses, the rest of the student body, along with all the faculty, parents, and friends who were in attendance—everyone in the building—joined in the singing. That stirred my heart even more! Now the entire building was reverberating with the fullness of our voices singing praises to Christ. All voices were singing. No one was silent.

That's the way it's going to be in Heaven one day. Beginning with those closest to the throne and then expanding outward, all creation will declare the lordship of Christ with increasing volume and passion. Every angel, whether elect angel or fallen demon—and every man, whether saved saint or lost sinner—will one day form one huge chorus and offer praise to Christ.

When all Heaven breaks loose!

So, how's your worship? Do you see yourself in the same spirit of worship as those around the throne?

SINGING IN THE REIGN

Ray Stedman, the noted pastor and author, once traveled to England to be the featured speaker at a Bible conference.

99

The sanctuary was unusually filled that night with people, eager to hear the Word of God preached by this renowned speaker. The chapel had never been so packed!

As the service began, the jubilant congregation was singing heartily to the Lord. You could just feel the Spirit's presence! One of the songs they were singing was the now popular—but then, unknown—chorus, "Our God Reigns."

Stedman was seated on the platform next to the host pastor, singing along with the congregation. As he looked down at the song sheet, he began to smile. Then chuckle. Finally, he began to laugh.

Why was Stedman laughing?

The words on the song sheet prepared for this special occasion had been mistyped. Instead of singing, "Our God reigns," the congregation was singing—at the very top of their lungs—"Our God resigns."

We laugh, but don't we do the same?

Although we probably have never sung those exact words, we have lived that way. When our world is turned upside-down, sometimes we live as if God has resigned and is no longer on the throne.

We need to see what John saw and remind ourselves that God is enthroned and reigning!

Let us never forget.

He's still on His throne!

Chapter Six

PARADISE REGAINED

The Re-Creation of Heaven

Revelation 21:1-8

⌢

*DON'T KNOW ABOUT YOUR FAMILY, BUT VACA-*tions around my house are bigger than life. They're like a Hollywood production. It takes us four days to pack and get our kids ready. By the time we load up our Suburban, we look like the Beverly Hillbillies with luggage and the important essentials (golf clubs) hanging out the rear window.

The highlight of the entire trip for me is pulling out of the driveway. You've got to understand that the main goal of the trip for me is just getting there. So, I'm not interested in stopping along the way for anything.

I don't think about bathroom breaks. I only stop for gas. In fact, our last car had a forty-gallon gas tank. We *never* had to stop for gas—*ever*.

My wife is constantly pleading with me on behalf of the kids to stop, let them go to the bathroom, stretch their legs, and have a break from being strapped into the car. So, *reluctantly*, I will stop just *once* for my family's sake at the halfway point.

That's what I want to do for you right now. We are now at the halfway point of this book, and I want to pull over and park for a second. I want to let you get out, stretch your legs, and catch your breath before we go any further.

So, where are we, anyway?

This is a book about *Heaven*. It's a book about being *heavenly minded* in the midst of our earthly pursuits. It's a book about focusing our lives upon things above where Christ is seated at God's right hand.

To this point, we have looked at Revelation 4 and 5 and gazed upon the focal point of Heaven—God's throne, occupied by God Himself and His Son, Jesus Christ. We have seen God in His glory, unveiled, undiminished, and unrivaled, and we have watched as all Heaven breaks loose in praise of our God.

We come now to the second half of our journey. We are ready to begin a new section in the book of Revelation, chapters 21 and 22. If Revelation 4 and 5 focuses upon the *Persons* of Heaven—God Himself and Jesus Christ—then Revelation 21 and 22 look at the *place* of Heaven itself—the new Jerusalem. These two sections serve as bookends of end-time events that will occur upon the earth (Revelation 6–20).

Right now, I am hitting the fast-forward button and speeding over the middle chapters of Revelation to get to the very end. We are cruising past the great tribulation (chapters 6–18), the Second Coming of Christ (chapter 19), and His millennial reign and final judgment (chapter 20) in order to get to the very end and return our thoughts to Heaven (Revelation 21–22).

This book is concerned with *Heaven*—the primacy of God and Jesus Christ in Heaven, the praise given them from those around the throne, the new Jerusalem where we will live forever, and our own personal preparation for eternity, right now!

So, let's think about what Heaven itself will be like. What will the new Jerusalem be like? More importantly, what will life be like in the celestial city?

No matter what "things" are in Heaven, it would still be Heaven just because God and Jesus Christ are there—period. It would be Heaven just to spend eternity with them, even if it we were to live there in a ghetto or slum. But in the final two chapters of Revelation, we discover that the description of Heaven itself is far more beautiful than we could ever imagine. What we will see is that Heaven is an actual place prepared by God for us (John 14:2-3).

As we now resume our journey through Heaven, you'd better prepare yourself. Because what John records will boggle our minds. This picture of Heaven far exceeds the grandest and most glorious thoughts we can imagine.

So, hop back in the car. Rebuckle your seat belt.

The journey reconvenes.

NEW, IMPROVED VERSION

John now introduces us to the final segment of his vision of Heaven. What he sees is *extraordinary*!

> *I saw a new heaven and a new earth; for the first heaven and the first earth passed away.* (Revelation 21:1)

Incredibly, John now becomes a firsthand spectator of the new Heaven and new earth. What John sees is breathtaking! Like nothing the human eye has ever seen before. John sees eternity and the future world to come.

The new Heaven that he sees is not new (*neos*) in time, but new in quality (*kainen*). John saw a new *kind* of Heaven—a new and improved version. One that is free from all defilement by Satan. One that has been purged by God's fiery judgment and regenerated by God's Spirit.

God will not annihilate the first creation and then create *ex nihilo* a second order. Rather, He will transform the first creation into a glorious new order.

The first heaven and earth, John says, will "pass away." This Greek word, *parer chommai*, does not mean extinction or annihilation, but transformation. It will be a dramatic change in quality from one level into a higher form.

For example, all Christians are a "new creation" in Christ. "Old things have passed away, behold, new things have come" (2 Corinthians 5:17). That doesn't mean that when we were converted to Christ we ceased to be, *per se*. I was not annihilated all together, but transformed from the inside-out. Likewise, the heavens and earth will be radically altered and gloriously reborn. This present universe will undergo a vast renovation—a rebirth or a remaking, if you will.

As we discussed in an earlier chapter, the Bible speaks of three heavens. There is the first heaven, which is the atmosphere around our world. The second heaven consists of the galaxies and planets. The third heaven is the throne room of God where He reigns above.

The recreation of a new Heaven refers to all three aspects. Everything—the atmosphere, the planets, and God's dwelling—will be recreated with supernatural splendor. God will upgrade all creation with glorious majesty and unspeakable beauty, beyond what our finite minds can even conceive!

Admittedly, the first creation isn't all bad. But, Satan's original rebellion in Heaven and his continued access before God's throne to accuse us has, in some way, defiled even God's dwelling place. Likewise, the earth's atmosphere has been contaminated because the devil is "the prince of the power of the air" (Ephesians 2:2). Trashy television programs and pornography, broadcast through the airwaves, has polluted even the air. But God will create a new Heaven—even all three heavens—free from the trace of any sin, one without stain or pollution. The whole universe will be dissolved and a new order created.

In this massive rebuilding project, God will also create a "new earth," as well. There are several Greek words for earth, or world. One word, *kosmos* means the world system (1 John 2:16), meaning the world of politics or the world of business, or the world of entertainment, etc. Such is man's ordered civilization that excludes God. Another word for the world, *aion*, means an era, or dispensation of time, an age or definite period of time. "I am with you always, even to the end of the age," meaning present world order (Matthew 28:20). Finally, the word *ge* means the physical earth upon which we live—the dirt, rocks, mountains, geography, geology.

It is this last word (*ge*) that John uses—the word that means the physical planet on which we live. There will be a new earth—one fit for eternity—with new rocks and trees, new mountains and rivers. A brand-new, improved earth.

God originally created this earth a paradise. The Garden of Eden was lush and beautiful, but sin turned the earth into a barren wilderness. Because of Adam's original sin, God pronounced a curse upon the earth (Genesis 3:17-19). Thus, the world became infested by thistles, thorns, and briers. Earthquakes and storms wreak havoc on this planet. Soil erosion, pollution, flash floods, droughts, and typhoons all defame God's creation.

THERE GOES THE NEIGHBORHOOD!

One day, God will create a new earth. He will restore this present wilderness back into a garden. Paradise lost—to borrow a phrase from John Milton—will become Paradise *regained*. It will be a new and improved version, infinitely more beautiful than the first Eden. A world pleasing to the senses. A virtual garden. A magnificent paradise. It will be gorgeous—with blooming flowers, bubbling streams, green hillsides, majestic mountains, rolling terrain, towering forests.

Whatever sin has touched and polluted, God will redeem and cleanse. If redemption does not go as far as the curse of sin, then God has failed. Whatever the extent of the consequences of sin, so must the extent of redemption be. Thus, even Heaven and earth must be purged and cleansed of the pollution of sin.

All this was foretold by the Old Testament prophets who looked ahead to this coming renovation. "Behold, I create new heavens and a new earth; and the former things shall not be remembered or come to mind" (Isaiah 65:17). The new Heaven and new earth will be so magnificent that no one will remember the first creation.

Again, Isaiah said, "The new heavens and the new earth which I make will endure before Me" (Isaiah 66:22).

The psalmist wrote of this future renovation. "Of old Thou didst found the earth; and the heavens are the work of Thy hands. Even they will perish, but Thou dost endure; and all of them will wear out like a garment; like clothing Thou wilt change them, and they will be changed" (Psalm 102:25-26). Just as easily as we take off an old, dirty shirt and put on a new, clean one, God will effortlessly change the present Heaven and earth.

Our Lord taught the same. "Heaven and earth will pass away, but My words shall not pass away" (Matthew 24:35).

106

The earth in its present form will one day pass away or change.

This present creation is under judgment, and God will one day destroy it with fire. After the destruction of the present universe, eternity will begin when God will create all things new.

The Apostle Paul agrees,

> *For the anxious longing of the creation waits eagerly for the revealing of the sons of God. For the creation was subjected to futility, not of its own will, but because of Him who subjected it, in hope that the creation itself also will be set free from its slavery to corruption into the freedom of the glory of the children of God. For we know that the whole creation groans and suffers the pains of childbirth together until now.* (Romans 8:19-22)

The writer of Hebrews says,

> *"Yet once more I will shake not only the earth, but also the heaven." And this expression, "yet once more," denotes the removing of those things which can be shaken, as of created things, in order that those things which cannot be shaken may remain.* (Hebrews 12:26-27)

The Apostle Peter concurs,

> *The present heavens and earth by His Word are being reserved for fire, kept for the day of judgment and destruction of ungodly men. . . . But the day of the Lord will come like a thief, in which the heavens will pass away with a roar and the elements will be destroyed with intense heat, and the earth and its works will be burned up. . . . But . . . we are looking for new heavens and a new earth in which righteousness dwells.* (2 Peter 3:7,10,13)

I CAN'T SEA IT ANYMORE!

Likewise, the new earth will no longer have any sea, oceans, nor any great bodies of water.

And there is no longer any sea. (Revelation 21:1)

If the heavens are literal, and the earth is literal—which I believe they are—then we can only assume that, within the same verse, the sea is also literal. There will be no literal sea in the new creation.

Many scientists who are Christians believe that before the great flood of Noah's day, there was no sea. But in the flood, the bottoms of the deep were opened up, allowing the release of great bodies of water, and the world was flooded. The oceans were then formed between the overturned land masses and the seas became a barrier separating what we now know to be continents, further dividing the human race. In the new earth, it appears there will be no sea because the earth will be restored to its original splendor.

Remember, at the time of this writing, John is exiled on Patmos, separated from his church by the Aegean Sea. For John, the sea was a painful barrier and wall of isolation from fellowship with his beloved flock.

To the ancient peoples, the sea was frightful and fearsome, an awesome monster, a watery grave. They had no compass to guide them in the open sea. On a cloudy day, their ships were absolutely lost without the stars or the sun to guide them. Their frail ships were at the mercy of the tempestuous ocean's fearsome, angry storms. The loss of human life in the sea was beyond calculation.

So the sea represented a vast barrier for nations, continents, and people groups. The sea was a separator of mankind around the globe. A destroyer of human life. But no more! No more geographical barriers to separate us. No more violent sea storms to bury victims in watery graves.

HERE COMES THE BRIDE!

John now sees another sight that must have startled him— like something out of a *Star Wars* movie.

I saw the holy city, new Jerusalem, coming down out of heaven from God, made ready as a bride adorned for her husband. (Revelation 21:2)

John saw a cubed city—as big as a continent—floating through space. He witnessed the holy city, the new Jerusalem, descending, coming down out of Heaven. This celestial city will be the eternal dwelling place for all believers. Here is a literal city with actual walls and gates, streets and buildings, rivers and trees (Revelation 21:9-21). Here is the final home of the saints, the heavenly city of God.

God has prepared this city to become the new capital of the eternal state. When the new Heaven and earth are recreated, then the new Jerusalem will come down out of the third heaven, where it will have completed construction.

When Jesus told His disciples that He was going to prepare a place for them (John 14:3), He was referring to this city. Now think about this! If Christ created this beautiful world in only six days, how awesome and stunning must this city be if He has been working on it two thousand years!

The writer of Hebrews described this city when he wrote, "The city which has foundations, whose architect and builder is God" (Hebrews 11:10). Also, this writer said, "But you have come to the city of the living God, the heavenly Jerusalem, and to myriads of angels, the general assembly and church of the first-born who are enrolled in heaven, and . . . God, the Judge of all, and . . . the spirits of righteous men made perfect" (12:22-23).

How does John see this city? He observes it traveling through space to hover over the earth like a suspended planet. He notes its sheer beauty, like "a bride adorned for her husband." I cannot think of a lovelier description than this. What prettier sight is there than a bride coming down the aisle?

As a pastor, I have performed *many* wedding ceremonies. One thing I can tell you—I have never yet seen an unattractive bride. Now, I have met with young women in premarital counseling *before* the wedding, and then I've seen her later *in* the wedding. Let me tell you, I can scarcely believe she is the *same* girl! At the moment of the wedding, I think God must somehow supernaturally transform *all* women with a glorious beauty that is God's alone. *Every* bride I've ever seen come down the aisle is beautiful!

I'm sure that's why John chose this imagery to describe to us the attractiveness of the new city. The celestial capital is just like a bride coming down the aisle for her husband— breathtaking in her beauty, heartstopping in her glory.

Who will live in this city? All the saints of all the ages will be there—Old Testament saints, as well as the Church throughout the centuries, will live together in glorious harmony.

FATHER OF THE BRIDE

Before John describes to us in detail the sheer beauty of the city itself—the golden streets and pearly gates—he first notes the most beautiful aspect of the city—God Himself! In this wedding, the Father of the bride outshines the bride.

> *And I heard a loud voice from the throne, saying, "Behold, the tabernacle of God is among men, and He shall dwell among them, and they shall be His people, and God Himself shall be among them."* (Revelation 21:3)

This loud voice is the voice of Christ Himself, the One who occupied the great white throne and judged the world (20:11). His voice is loud because His words are authoritative, commanding, and extremely important. Jesus announces that the tabernacle of God is now among men.

What He tells us is that God will move into this city and live with all believers in intimate, continuous fellowship. He will commune with us forever!

The tabernacle of God is the place of His holy abode among His people. In past days, the Lord tabernacled— abided—with humankind. First, He tabernacled with Adam and Eve in the garden in close, intimate fellowship. Second, God tabernacled with the patriarchs. He spoke directly to Abraham as a man would talk to His friend, face-to-face. Then the Lord tabernacled with Israel in the wilderness where He appeared as a pillar of fire by night and as a cloud by day. Fourth, He tabernacled in the temple in Jerusalem. He dwelt in the darkness of the Holy of Holies. Next, God tabernacled in a human body as "the Word became flesh and dwelt [tabernacled] among us" (John 1:14). Today, the Lord tabernacles in His Church as He indwells our hearts by the Holy Spirit. But in the eternal state, He will far more fully and visibly tabernacle among us! God Himself will live in our midst!

Specifically, God's immediate presence will be with His people. This pictures His close fellowship in Heaven with us, His people (Revelation 13:6, 15:5). Our eyes will see Him! Our ears will hear Him! We will behold His glory!

In Heaven, we will never leave His presence—*never!* John already informed us, "They are before the throne of God; and they serve Him day and night in His temple; and He who sits on the throne shall spread His tabernacle over them" (Revelation 7:15). Here is the closeness of His fellowship with us. The tabernacle of His presence will always overshadow us.

This is where we fulfill our destiny. Man was designed to live in the immediate presence of God and to enjoy Him face-to-face. The curse of sin banished us from His presence. But in this final salvation, the last effect of the curse is removed. "He shall dwell among them, and they shall be His people, and God Himself shall be among them" (Revelation 21:3).

Why does this verse say God *Himself?* Isn't it enough to say *God* shall be among them? *Himself* is emphatic. This is not merely His representative or delegate—but God *Himself!*

NO MORE TEARS

As long as we live in this sinful world, sorrow will cloud our hearts and tears will ill our eyes. Until the moment we enter the gates of Heaven, God's people will feel the pain of living in a sinful world. We may forget how to laugh, but we will never forget how to cry. Not until we enter the new Jerusalem.

Suffering is a universal language, the common denominator of human life. It will only be there, beyond the pearly gates and jasper walls, that the Lord will—once and for all—wipe away our tears. John writes:

*And He shall wipe away every tear from their eyes; and
there shall no longer be any death; there shall no longer
be any mourning, or crying, or pain; the first things have
passed away. And He who sits on the throne said,
"Behold, I am making all things new."* (Revelation 21:4-5)

In the new Jerusalem, there will not be any more tears.
Our tears, caused by grief and pain, will be no more. *Every*
tear focuses upon God's great compassion for us, His own
children. His concern is infinitely minute. This means every
single tear will be wiped away, never to well up and roll
down our trembling cheeks again.

There is no sense of need. No wanting for anything. No
negative emotion.

"Earth has no sorrow that heaven cannot heal," wrote
Thomas Moore, nineteenth-century Irish poet.[1]

There is many a broken heart in this world, but not in
the new Jerusalem. There will no longer be any tears because
there will no longer be any causes for crying. No death, no
pain, no strife.

In the eternal state, death will be a thing of the past.
There will be no graves in the hillside of Heaven. No obitu-
ary columns. No funeral processions over the streets of gold.

There will be no sorrow. We will never hear any wailing. Only joy and happiness. Our bliss will be far beyond
our greatest merriment today. We will experience deepest
joy, merriest laughter, fullest bliss. Our broken hearts will be
mended and our aching bodies forever healed. We will
experience infinite blessedness beyond our current ability
to measure.

Here are the reasons for the disappearance of death.
Here is why all sorrow, crying, and pain will pass away.
Because "the first things have passed away." This old creation with its present world order, ravaged by the inestimable damage of sin, will be done away with.

We cannot imagine what it will be like. Even this
present world, marred and spoiled by sin, contains scenes
of beauty that take our breath away. But in that day, the
Lord Jesus will exert the genius of His creative imagination

and refurnish a new Heaven and new earth with the extraordinary resources of His unlimited power! Here is the exercise of His power, riches, wisdom, and might that He received when He took the scroll (Revelation 5:12).

MEMBERS ONLY

Mark Twain once said, "I'll take heaven for its climate and hell for its company."[2] Well then, who is the company of hell? Who is it that Mr. Twain desires to fellowship with? Let's take a look at the roll call of the damned.

> *But for the cowardly and unbelieving and abominable and murderers and immoral persons and sorcerers and idolaters and all liars, their part will be in the lake that burns with fire and brimstone, which is the second death.*
> (Revelation 21:8)

These kinds of vile, perverse persons have made our cities concentrated centers of wickedness. Go to the downtown sections of major cities and the ravaged streets at night are crawling with such people. But these people will be banned from the heavenly city to come. Sin has wrecked and ruined our major cities. But God will *not* let it ruin the new Jerusalem. The ungodly will *not* intermingle with believers in this new city.

Charles Ryrie said, "People who are characterized by any of these eight traits listed here will be in the lake of fire, and, thus, excluded from heaven. Notice that the text does not say that anyone who has ever committed any of these sins will be excluded, but people whose lives are characterized in these ways. There is a difference, for instance, in ever telling a lie and being a liar as the habit of one's life."[3]

Let's look at these lifestyles one by one. As we do, remember that it is only by the grace of God that any of us will be admitted into God's presence. We are all sinners who have missed the mark and fallen short of God's perfect standard of righteousness. None of us deserves Heaven. It is only by His grace that we shall enter.

Nevertheless, true conversion brings about a trans-

113

formation of life. When Christ comes into our hearts by
faith, we are never the same again. Our feet are put onto a
new path—a narrow path that leads to life (Matthew 7:14).

This does not mean we never sin again. But it does
mean that we will no longer habitually practice—day in,
day out—the same sins in an unrepentant lifestyle (1 John
3:9). The bent and direction of our lives will now be marked
by the pursuit of holiness (Hebrews 12:14)—all a work of
His grace (1 Corinthians 15:10).

Now, here are the main categories of who never had
their lives changed and will never enter Heaven.

First, *the cowardly*—literally, the fearful—will be banned.
These are people who verbally profess Christ ("Many will
say to me on that day, 'Lord, Lord'" [Matthew 7:22]), but
who recant when persecuted for Christ (13:21). These are
"false" believers who profess Christ but fall away under the
world's persecution of Christianity. They made some kind
of outward testimony for Christ, but they were never truly
born again. When confronted and opposed by the world,
they draw back in fear, demonstrating that they were never
saved to begin with. "But My righteous one shall live by
faith; and if he shrinks back, My soul has no pleasure in
him" (Hebrews 10:38).

Conversely, true believers are bold in the Holy Spirit.
"For God has not given us a spirit of timidity, but of power
and love and discipline" (2 Timothy 1:7).

Second, *the unbelieving*—literally, the faithless ones—
will be excluded. These are disloyal to Christ and eventually
withdraw and deny their faith in Christ (John 6:66). But
those genuinely converted will persevere in their faith. Paul
makes this clear: "Yet He has now reconciled you in His
fleshly body through death, in order to present you before
Him holy and blameless and beyond reproach—if indeed
you continue in the faith firmly established and steadfast,
and not moved away from the hope of the gospel that you
have heard" (Colossians 1:22-23).

Third, *the abominable*—literally, those polluted by sin—
will be shut out. Here are those defiled by the world system
and the flesh. Those who have been perverted with any-

thing contrary to God's Holy Word. "Nothing unclean and no one who practices abomination . . . shall ever come into it" (Revelation 21:27).

Those squeezed into the world's mold (Romans 12:2) will never fit through the narrow gate of Heaven (Matthew 7:14). Those who habitually love this world have never received the love of God (1 John 2:15). Paul says, "They profess to know God, but by their deeds they deny Him, being detestable and disobedient, and worthless for any good deed" (Titus 1:16).

Fourth, *no murderers* will be admitted, specifically those guilty of persecuting and martyring Christians. Those violent killers for whom the lives of other humans have very little or no value—gang members, thieves, abortionists—will be forever banished from Heaven.

It is these murderers to whom John refers, "I saw underneath the altar [in heaven] the souls of those who had been slain because of the word of God and because of the testimony which they had maintained" (Revelation 6:9). "They poured out the blood of saints and prophets" (16:6). "I saw the woman [Babylon] drunk with the blood of the saints and with the blood of the witnesses of Jesus" (17:6). "And in her was found the blood of prophets and of saints and of all who have been slain on the earth" (18:24). The blood of believers is a picture of this world's gross hatred of God running its full course and vented against His children.

Fifth, *no immoral person* shall enter Heaven. Those caught up in sexual perversions—adultery, homosexuality, lesbianism, pornography—shall be forever excluded. Only the pure in heart shall see God (Matthew 5:8).

Sixth, *all sorcerers* will be denied access. Those entangled with mystical spiritism through pagan magic, mind-altering drugs, demonic seances, satanic witchcraft, and evil incantations, John writes, will never enter Heaven.

Seventh, *all idolaters* will be kept out. This refers to anyone who habitually puts anything before God. It may be the idolatry of materialism (Colossians 3:5)—just ask the rich young ruler (Matthew 19:16-22)—or any other earthly pursuit put before the pursuit of God.

Finally, *no liars* will ever be admitted. Liars are those who deny Christ and turn to the religious lies of false teachers and embrace their damnable religion. Jesus revealed Himself as "the way, and the *truth*, and the life" (John 14:6)—no one comes to God apart from His truth. Anyone who believes a lie contrary to God's truth is a liar—one who is identified with the devil's lies. Likewise, these liars lack the integrity of truthfulness and bear false witness.

By sharp contrast, of the 144,000 truly converted in the last days, it is said, "No lie was found in their mouth; they are blameless" (Revelation 14:5).

The eternal destiny of all these Christ-rejecting sinners will be the lake that burns with fire and brimstone. Brimstone is sulfuric acid that burns, a well-known instrument of God's wrath used previously in the judgment of Sodom and Gomorrah. This is the second death—the eternal separation of the lost from God forever. All these mentioned— the cowardly, unbelieving, abominable, murderers, immoral, sorcerers, idolaters, and liars—will *not* be admitted into Heaven.

So, who will be in Heaven? The humblest sinner who repents, that is who will be there. All who put personal faith in Christ alone will be privileged members of the royal family there.

HEAVEN, HELP US!

What should these verses about a new Heaven and new earth say to us today? Plenty. Here are truths that should have a profound effect upon our daily lives.

First, *here is a call to encouragement.* No matter how discouraging your present hour, Heaven tells us that there is a better day coming. You and I can endure our present trials, no matter how hot the flames, knowing that eternal rest and divine relief are right before us.

Are you weary? Have you suffered disappointment? Discouragement? Are you tired from the heavy burdens of this life? Are there tears in your eyes? Tears from physical affliction? From the loss of loved ones? Do you mourn over your indwelling sin?

116

Be assured that a better day is coming. A day when God will wipe away every tear from your eyes. A day when He will personally comfort you. A day when He will remove sin, sorrow, and death from your life.

Second, here is a call to evangelism. We must tell everyone we meet that Heaven is a real place and that the way is provided through Christ alone. Every man and woman has within them, instinctively, the longing to go to Heaven. Only the Bible tells us how to get there. Let us be a mouthpiece for Christ, sharing the good news.

Do you know someone who needs to go to Heaven? Then go tell them!

Third, here is a call to examination. Are you sure you are going to Heaven? When the roll is called up yonder, do you know that you will be there? Have you trusted in Christ alone for your salvation? Have you repented of your sins? Have you? Has your life been changed? Have you been reborn?

Many people will miss Heaven by eighteen inches—the distance between their heads and their hearts. Make certain that Christ is in your heart by faith.

The Bible says that God is holy and your sin has forever separated you from Him—the very One you were created to know and enjoy. But God, being gracious, has provided the way back to Him. He sent His only begotten Son to bear your sin (Isaiah 53:4-6). Jesus died the death you deserve because of your sins. Triumphantly, He was raised again and lives to save all who call upon Him.

If you will turn to Christ today and commit your life to Him by faith, He will pardon you and reconcile you to God.

Repent of your sins.

Receive Him as your Lord and Savior today.

NOTES

1. Thomas Moore, source unknown.
2. Mark Twain, quoted by Adrian Rogers, "The Roll Call of the Damned," unpublished manuscript on Revelation 21:8.
3. Charles Ryrie, Revelation (Chicago, IL: Moody, 1979), page 120.

Chapter Seven

IT *JUST* DOESN'T GET ANY BETTER THAN THIS!

The Grandeur of Heaven

Revelation 21:9-21

HERE ARE MANSIONS—AND THEN THERE ARE MANSIONS. George Vanderbilt definitely built a *mansion*.

The grandson of railroad industrialist and financier "Commandore" Vanderbilt, George Washington Vanderbilt III set out to build the grandest home in America. Armed with an unlimited budget, the result was mind-boggling.

In 1888, the thirty-three-year-old Vanderbilt began purchasing large parcels of land in Asheville, North Carolina—including the 100,000-acre Pisgah Forest for his backyard! He then commissioned two of the most distinguished architects of his time—the famous building architect Richard Morris Hunt and noted landscape architect Frederick Law Olmstead—to design this superstructure and the surrounding grounds called the Biltmore Estate.

Rivaling the grandest manors of Europe, this house was designed to be a four-story stone edifice with a 780-foot-long facade. The construction required over a thousand workers. Countless tons of materials were used. Limestone was hauled in from six hundred miles away in Indiana. Marble was imported from Italy. The delivery of such elaborate materials required a specially built private railroad spur. Thirty-two thousand bricks were made on site daily. A woodworking factory was built just to process the oak and walnut timber for the floors and paneling.

For six years, an army of skilled workers labored to create this country estate, a self-contained community in the Smoky Mountains.

On Christmas Eve, 1895, George Vanderbilt unveiled his prized Biltmore House. As he welcomed family and friends for a holiday celebration, Vanderbilt formally opened the most ambitious home ever constructed in America.

A walk through this mansion reveals a house beyond anyone's wildest imagination. It boasts four acres of floor space, a total of 250 rooms. Thirty-four master bedrooms. Forty-three bathrooms. Sixty-five fireplaces. Three kitchens. An indoor swimming pool. And a gymnasium. It was maintained by a staff of eighty who also lived in the house.

The Biltmore mansion was immediately acclaimed the greatest house of the Western Hemisphere. The youngest in a family known internationally for building palatial homes, George Vanderbilt had truly outdone them all.

But, let's face it: Despite its opulent grandeur, even the Biltmore Estate pales in comparison to the architectural accomplishments of Jesus Christ in Heaven.

In the unseen world above, Jesus is building a mansion that will overshadow anything ever built by human hands. Christ said, "In my Father's house are many dwelling places; if it were not so, I would have told you; for I go to prepare a place for you. And if I go and prepare a place for you, I will come again, and receive you to Myself; that where I am, there you may be also" (John 14:2-3).

There are mansions—and then there are *mansions*.

Jesus Christ is building a *mansion*.

People who are heavenly minded are looking forward with great eagerness to occupying this mansion in glory. While so many are preoccupied with larger or better earthly houses, the one who is heavenly minded will be focused upon his heavenly home.

What kind of place is Jesus preparing? How does it compare to the finest estates of this world? With what materials will Jesus build His mansion? What will be the measurements of His heavenly home?

The answers to these questions, and more, are found in the next installment of John's vision of Heaven recorded in Revelation 21:9-21. Let's take a further look at our celestial home above.

A GEM OF A CITY

First and foremost, John is struck by the sheer glory of God's dwelling place. The chief characteristic of the new Jerusalem is that God's glory is manifest in it.

> *One of the seven angels who had the seven bowls full of the seven last plagues, came and spoke with me, saying, "Come here, I shall show you the bride, the wife of the Lamb." And he carried me away in the Spirit to a great and high mountain, and showed me the holy city, Jerusalem, coming down out of heaven from God, having the glory of God. Her brilliance was like a very costly stone, as a stone of crystal-clear jasper.* (Revelation 21:9-11)

A solitary angel—one of the seven who dispense God's wrath during the Tribulation—summoned John to embark upon a careful inspection of the eternal city. Supernaturally, unexplainably, the angel transported John in a state of prophetic ecstasy to a great mountain. From this high vantage point, the apostle can see the vast magnitude of the city more clearly.

What strikes his attention first? This city shines like a celestial jewel with blinding brilliance. God's glory (*doxa*) is the radiance of His dazzling splendor, the abiding Shekinah glory of God. This imagery is beyond anything a Stephen Spielberg movie could create with all the latest special effects.

In Scripture, whenever God revealed Himself to His people, He appeared in the form of the Shekinah—a brilliant, almost blinding light. In the Old Testament, the Shekinah was the symbol of the sum of all that God is—the brilliant outshining of the totality of His attributes and His nature. God, in all of His perfection, is so brilliant and dazzling that He is blinding!

The celestial city's brilliance, or bright light, is the effect of the divine glory shining throughout the city—a shimmering radiance and eternal effulgence. Her beauty resembles a sparkling crystal, diamond-like stone blazing with the glory of God—extremely beautiful, costly, and valuable.

This precious stone, a "crystal-clear jasper," is an opaque quartz found in various colors. This probably refers to a perfectly cut diamond that magnifies the brilliant light of God's glory. Like a costly gem, the city is transparent, gleaming, and refracting light, reflecting all the colors of the rainbow. It is pure, clear, white, bright, blindingly brilliant, starry, projecting a diamond-like radiance that magnifies the light of God's radiant glory. God's glory covers the infinite universe with breathtaking beauty.

The building materials of Heaven are selected with a view to magnify the glory of God. Not one of these materials is brilliant in the dark. In any context, their radiance is always dependent upon borrowed light. Here, the light is the dazzling glory of God. All of Heaven is designed to magnify and show off the glory of God. "And the city has no need of the sun or of the moon to shine upon it, for the glory of God has illumined it, and its lamp is the Lamb" (Revelation 21:23).

"WALL-TO-WALL" GLORY

Let's continue the tour of Heaven. Surrounding the celestial city is a massive wall, symbolizing security and protection. John records:

It had a great and high wall. (Revelation 21:12)

In the ancient world, a city's wall was a source of protection from external danger and harmful attacks. Likewise, the city's wall promoted closeness among the indwelling inhabitants. In God's city, the wall will serve as an eternal reminder to His people that they have been delivered from the danger of any external foe or invading enemy that would harm them. The wall symbolizes the protection that believers will enjoy from all their spiritual enemies—Satan, demons, sin, sinners, death, disease, sorrow, and pain. Nothing that could harm us will ever break into the celestial city!

John gives specifics about the wall in a few verses. Amazingly, this wall is comprised of twelve foundation stones (verse 14) and twelve names of the apostles (verse 14);

it is seventy-two yards thick (verse 17), made of jasper (verse 18), has twelve foundation stones of every kind (verses 19-20), and we enter through twelve gates of pearl (verse 21).

This is quite a wall!

THROUGH GATES OF SPLENDOR

This great and high wall has twelve gates, which accommodate unrestricted entrance into the city for God's people when opened. Likewise, these gates keep others out when shut. John's account continues:

> *It had a great and high wall, with twelve gates, and at the gates twelve angels; and names were written on them, which are those of the twelve tribes of the sons of Israel. There were three gates on the east and three gates on the north and three gates on the south and three gates on the west. And the wall of the city had twelve foundation stones, and on them were the twelve names of the twelve apostles of the Lamb.* (Revelation 21:12-14)

Gates are entrance places and exit points, allowing travel in and out of the new Jerusalem. Apparently, believers will travel through these gates to leave the city to far-away points of the vast recreated universe. We will not be confined within these walls throughout eternity. Instead, we will be free to travel to other parts of the new heavens and the new earth. We will journey to the outer confines of God's universe—perhaps to other planets—in order to minister and to serve Him. We will repeatedly enter through these gates to worship God, fellowship with other believers, and then exit again to serve Him.

Our glorified bodies will have unlimited capacities to travel. For example, after His resurrection, Jesus suddenly and mysteriously appeared in the upper room to His disciples. He passed right through the walls! In our glorified bodies, we will have the same capacity to travel through space and instantly appear in another part of God's new creation. There will be no speed limit in Heaven! You will finally be able to push the pedal to the metal and travel fast.

The new universe will be as big, if not bigger, than it is now, and vastly more glorious and beautiful. We will travel throughout the *infinite* outer space and see it all.

Presently, scientists tell us there are billions of galaxies, each containing billions of stars like our own sun. Each of these billions of stars may be encircled by its own solar system of planets—perhaps countless earthlike planets! There will be new and unlimited worlds for us to discover, encounter, explore, develop, and experience!

Perhaps we'll serve God for a few million years on one planet and, wanting a change of scenery, fly off to another one of a billion trillion planets to explore and develop for a few million years.

Each of these twelve gates is guarded by twelve angels, one angel per gate. Isaiah wrote, "On your walls, O Jerusalem, I have appointed watchmen; all day and night they will never keep silent" (62:6).

Each gate contains a name of one of the twelve tribes of Israel. Even in eternity, Israel and the Church are distinguished, though both comprise one body of God's redeemed people.

There are three gates on the east, three on the north, three on the south, and three on the west. Thus, the city is a perfect square, or perhaps rectangular. At its base, it is four-sided, at perfect ninety-degree angles, with three gates on each of its four sides.

The wall of the city has twelve foundation stones upon which the entire city rests. On these stones are the twelve names of the twelve apostles. The mention of the Twelve reminds the city dwellers of the apostles' connection with the foundation of the Church. Paul writes, "Having been built upon the foundation of the apostles and prophets, Christ Jesus Himself being the corner stone" (Ephesians 2:20).

TAPE MEASURE, PLEASE

Next, John notes that the city is a perfectly symmetrical, fifteen hundred-mile cube, reflecting the triunity (height, length, and breadth) and perfection of God.

And the one who spoke with me had a gold measuring rod to measure the city, and its gates and its wall. And the city is laid out as a square, and its length is as great as the width; and he measured the city with the rod, fifteen hundred miles; its length and width and height are equal. And he measured its wall, seventy-two yards, according to human measurements, which are also angelic measurements. (Revelation 21:15-17)

The angel, the one who was giving John the guided tour, had a gold measuring rod in his hand. This rod was used to measure the holy city, its gates, and its wall. This measurement was a sign of ownership, showing that the city belonged to God.

Earlier in Revelation, a measuring rod was given to John and he was told to measure the earthly Jerusalem, signifying that it uniquely belonged to God (Revelation 11:1). Jerusalem is God's own special possession. He will do a special work of grace within its parameters. Previously, John was told *not* to measure the outer court of the Gentiles (verse 2). This request signifies that this city belongs to God! He alone is the divine Architect and Builder. It is indwelt exclusively by His people. Within its confines, He performs a special work of grace.

Furthermore, this precise measurement conveys conformity to perfection. It is measured to determine that this city meets God's specifications perfectly. Because God is perfectly holy, even His holy city is perfectly conformed to a standard.

The city seems to be laid out as a square, perfectly equal on all sides. Its length, width, and height are equal. Thus, it is either a perfect cube, or possibly a pyramid—perfectly symmetrical, perfectly balanced, reflecting the perfectly symmetrical triunity of God.

Because God is thrice holy, this city is, correspondingly, equal in its length, width, and height. No dimension of the city is out of balance because there is no attribute of God out of balance. All His works and ways are perfectly in order.

"God is not a God of confusion [disorder] but of peace [wholeness]" (1 Corinthians 14:33).

This symmetry also symbolizes the perfect harmony within the Godhead. Our triune God works together in perfect unison—God the Father, God the Son, and God the Holy Spirit working perfectly together.

The angel measured the city with the rod. It was 1,500 miles wide, 1,500 miles long, and 1,500 miles high, or 2,250,000 square miles at the base and height. This is huge! But it's commensurate with the importance of this noted city. The dimensions of the new Jerusalem are the size of an area from Florida to Maine to Minneapolis to Houston. Or, picture an area in the western United States between the Pacific Coast and the Mississippi River, roughly the distance from Los Angeles to Saint Louis. Or New York to Denver. The size of this city is staggering.

And the city is this same distance high!

Let's face it, God can never be accused of skimping or economizing. Here He builds a magnificent city fully capable of holding the vast population of redeemed saints and elect angels.

Notice the dimensions of the city's wall, which frames or defines the outer circumference. He measured its wall to be seventy-two yards. This probably refers to the width of the wall. If this were the height, 216 feet would be a small fraction of the seven-million-foot (that's 7,000,000 feet high!) height of the city. But the thickness would not be out of proportion to the extreme height of the wall.

John says that this was "according to human measurements, which were also angelic measurements." That means that though measured by an angel, a human standard was employed. Its figures are determined by standards common among men. Further, this statement by John—"according to human measurements"—means this description is to be taken quite literally. The city is not just a symbol of eternal bliss or some ethereal world we enter into with God. God Himself has designed a real place for His eternal dwelling where He can enjoy His people. All the major orthodox commentators and scholars agree on the literal nature of Heaven described in Revelation 21–22.

Will there be enough room for everyone in the new Jerusalem? Will we be too crowded to enjoy it? No way! There will be plenty of room! The city is 1,500 miles in every direction. That's 2,250,000 square miles, on the ground. Then 1,500 miles up from there! Hang on! Are you ready for this? That's 3,375,000,000 cubic miles, enough room to comfortably accommodate 100,000 billion people!

It has been estimated that approximately thirty billion people have lived in the long history of the world. Even if everyone who ever lived was saved—which is not the case—that would still allow each person 200 square miles on the ground alone. If only half were saved, that would be 400 square miles per person. And that's not even considering the cubic miles! The point is, there will be plenty of room for everyone who makes it to Heaven.

And that's just the city! We will have trillions and bezillions of miles of new heavens to explore! The plural of the term *heavens* symbolizes the vastness of the new creation. This place is going to be—as my sons would say—"Mega-awesome!"

NOTHING BUT THE BEST

John now describes the materials with which the new Jerusalem is constructed. No cheap stuff here! No budget cutbacks on this building program. Only the best for God!

No cinder blocks. No shag carpeting. God wants to make a statement. He wants to reveal His greatness. There's no getting the wrong idea of God here! So John describes the materials used for the wall, the city, the foundation stones, the gates, and the street. Get out your calculators! There was no finance committee. The new Jerusalem is a *budget-buster*!

> *And the material of the wall was jasper; and the city was pure gold, like clear glass. The foundation stones of the city wall were adorned with every kind of precious stone. The first foundation stone was jasper; the second, sap-*

*phire; the third, chalcedony; the fourth, emerald; the fifth,
sardonyx; the sixth, sardius; the seventh, chrysolite; the
eighth, beryl; the ninth, topaz; the tenth, chrysoprase; the
eleventh, jacinth; the twelfth, amethyst. And the twelve
gates were twelve pearls; each one of the gates was a
single pearl, and the street of the city was pure gold,
like transparent glass.* (Revelation 21:18-21)

The material of the wall surrounding the city is jasper,
the most beautiful gem, and the city itself is pure gold, like
clear glass.

In the city of Dallas, on the southeast corner of the
intersection of its infamous Central Expressway (I-75 North)
and Northwest Highway (Loop 12) is a building made of real
gold. Literally! The Fina Building—also called Campbell
Centre—was constructed back in the early 1970s before the
price of gold went through the roof. It was only thirty-two
dollars per ounce back then.

So the architects down in oil-rich Dallas thought, "Let's
build a gold metal flake building."

The building is constructed like any other fine office
complex, except the glass that forms its entire outer shell is
filled with gold metal flake. When the sun is fading in the
west, the glare from the building can blind the unsuspect-
ing motorists heading home in five o'clock traffic!

Its brilliance is unsurpassed! But this is a mere foretaste
of the gold—not gold-filled, but solid, pure gold!—of the
heavenly city.

The celestial skyline is aglow with the glory of God. It
shines because it is one mass of gold, emitting a dazzling
luster. Here is gold so pure that it surpasses any gold belonging to this old creation. The tops of the visible buildings,
towers, and roofs reflect God's splendor.

J. Vernon McGee offers an interesting perspective here.
He writes, "Think of the city as a cube within a crystal-clear
sphere. What we are given are the *inside* measurements. I
think of it as a big plastic ball with a cube inside, having all
eight of its corners touching the sphere. To enclose a cube
measuring 1,500 miles on each side, the circumference of

the sphere would be about 8,164 miles. The diameter of the moon is about 2,160 miles, and that of the New Jerusalem will be somewhat larger than the moon, and it will be a sphere like the other heavenly bodies."[1]

If McGee is correct, this would be a golden-domed enclosure around the city. Otherwise, the gold is the material of the buildings. But either way, it will be stunning!

NO BARGAIN-BASEMENT SPECIAL

The foundation stones support the entire city wall. This does not mean that the foundations were decorated with these stones, but that they consisted of the very stones themselves.

They were adorned with every variety of precious, valuable stones. Twelve are now listed for us. Interestingly, eight of the twelve correspond to the stones in the breastplate of Israel's high priest (see also Exodus 28, 39). Also, there is some correspondence here with the stones around God's throne (Revelation 4:3).

These stones are different colors with great variety in their shade, brilliance, and hue—blue (sapphire), green (chalcedony, emerald, beryl, chrysoprase), red (sardius), yellow (chrysolite), clear (jasper), gold (chrysolite, topaz), purple (jacinth, amethyst), and white (sardonyx).

The first foundation stone represents the first layer of the foundation. The whole city rests upon these foundation stones. Think of the dazzling colors! The first stone is jasper or diamond, crystal-clear, white. The second is sapphire, blue in color, or sky-blue flecked with gold. The third is chalcedony, possibly a green silicate of copper or an agate, greenish, a variety of emerald. The fourth, an emerald. The fifth, sardonyx, is white with layers of red. The sixth, sardius, is fiery red. The seventh stone, chrysolite, has a golden hue, yellow. The eighth, beryl, is sea-green, emerald-like. The ninth, topaz, is golden green, perhaps a greenish yellow. The tenth, chrysoprase, is a translucent, golden-green, paler green than the beryl. The eleventh, jacinth, is violet. The twelfth stone, amethyst, is a vivid violet, a purplish color more brilliant than the violet jacinth.

The very foundations of this celestial city are constructed on the flashing brilliance of rich and costly gems. This will be the most breathtaking sight we will ever see— except for the direct glory of God Himself.

The new Jerusalem is a city of light—the light which is the glory of God. Therefore, it is a city of color. That's because color is actually nothing more than dissected light. Where there is no light, there is no color. Objects reveal color according to their ability to absorb or to reject light rays. For example, a red stone absorbs all the color rays except red. It rejects or throws back to the eye the red ray, which gives it the color of red.

What's the point?

Everything about the heavenly city is designed to display the glory of God. So it will be in the new order of creation, but to a much more intense degree. On the inside of this city is Jesus Christ—the Light of the world (John 8:12). There, He will be the Light of the universe. Because of His bright shining presence—so bright that there will be no need for the sun—all of this color will be flooding out of the new Jerusalem and illuminating the entire universe.

The glory of God has always taken center stage. It was primary in the old created order—"the heavens are telling of the glory of God" (Psalm 19:1); "The whole earth is full of His glory" (Isaiah 6:3). And it will be central in the new creation.

PORTALS OF GLORY

The twelve gates are made of a dozen pearls, each entrance a single pearl. What diamonds are to modern culture, pearls were to the ancient world. Among the ancients, the pearl was highest in value among the precious stones. His beauty is due entirely to God's work—just like the new Jerusalem. Improvement by human workmanship is impossible.

The pearl was among the most treasured ornaments of the wealthier class—one of the most valuable items in the Roman world (1 Timothy 2:9). In New Testament times, the merchant who dealt with pearls was well-known. So Jesus said that gaining the Kingdom of Heaven is like a merchant acquiring a fine pearl to resell in the marketplace. It will require selling all that you possess in order to purchase one pearl of great value (Matthew 13:45-46). Our Lord also said that the infinite, unfathomable riches of the gospel was like a pearl not to be thrown away before swine (Matthew 7:6). And Paul said that women were not to come to church with a gaudy display of distracting wealth, like wearing pearls (1 Timothy 2:9).

Each gate tower is carved from a single, huge pearl. Why did God choose pearl? Perhaps because the beauty of a pearl comes from the pain of an oyster. It is beauty born out of pain. A pearl is formed when a tiny grain of sand gets inside an oyster's shell, causing the oyster to become irritated and uncomfortable. The oyster relieves its pain by covering the irritating grain of sand with a soft, lustrous solution that hardens into a beautiful, growing pearl. The more pain the oyster endures, the more layers of lustre, and the larger the pearl becomes.

What a picture of our salvation! We have come into the place of God's blessing out of the pain of Christ at the cross.

John Phillips writes, "How appropriate! All other precious gems are metals or stones, but a pearl is a gem formed within the oyster—the only one formed by living flesh. The humble oyster receives an irritation or a wound, and around the offending article that has penetrated and hurt it, the oyster builds a pearl. The pearl, we might say, is the answer of the oyster to that which injured it."

"The glory land," Phillips continues, "is God's answer, in Christ, to wicked men who crucified heaven's beloved and put Him to open shame. How like God it is to build the gates of the new Jerusalem of pearl. The saints, as they come and go, will be forever reminded, as they pass the gates of glory, that access to God's home is only because of Calvary. Think of the size of those gates! Think of the supernatural pearls from which they are made! What gigantic suffering is symbolized by those gates of pearl! Throughout the endless ages we shall be reminded by those pearly gates of the immensity of the sufferings of Christ. Those pearls, hung eternally at the access routes to glory, will remind us forever of One who hung upon a tree and whose answer to those who injured Him was to invite them to share His home. "[2]

TWENTY-FOUR–CARAT SUPER-HIGHWAY

The streets of the city are pure gold, like transparent glass. An entire network of super-highways will crisscross the city, taking travelers to all points of the celestial community. In the very center, there is one main avenue proceeding directly to the throne of God.

In the typical ancient city, the main street led from the entrance gate of the city to the central temple or palace. In the new Jerusalem, this street of gold is the broad thoroughfare of busy activity and heavy traffic, accommodating worshipers in Heaven with access to God's throne.

This heavenly highway system is pure gold, costly and valuable, reflecting the divine nature of its Architect. The gold is like transparent glass, allowing God's light to flood through it. Again, this will further amplify and magnify the glory of God. It will enhance the display of His majesty and stir our hearts to worship Him.

HOME IMPROVEMENTS . . . NOW!

This is where we will spend all eternity. Talk about moving up to a better neighborhood! How glorious will be our eternal dwelling place! What eternal impact this truth should have upon us today!

First, *the glory of this city should give us a present contentment with what we have in this world.* Seeing such a bright future ought to make us satisfied with what we now possess and where we live, knowing that one day we will be moving into such a glorious home.

That was Paul's perspective. "For I consider that the sufferings of this present time are not worthy to be compared with the glory that is to be revealed to us" (Romans 8:18). We can be content with present suffering and personal shortages knowing that such an incredible future awaits us.

Second, *we learn much about God by looking at His celestial home.* His fingerprints are all over the celestial city, revealing His holy character to all who see it.

What have we learned about the city of God?

The new Jerusalem is full of bright light. Surrounded by a great wall. Accessed by twelve gates of pearl. Guarded by twelve angels. Supported by twelve foundation stones. Laid out as a square cube. Built according to specific measurements. Encompassing immense proportions of space. Encircled with gold. Adorned with precious stones like jasper, sapphire, emerald, sardius, and topaz. Networked by a golden street.

So, what does this tell us about God?

Clearly, this city tells us that God is a God of inestimable beauty and glory. He is a God of royal pomp and fabulous wealth. A God of precise order, structure, and majesty. A God of accessibility and openness. A God who operates by set standards. A God of unimaginable extravagance, splendor, and creativity. A God of perfect peace, opulent grandeur, and lavishness.

The character of God is definitely reflected in His heavenly dwelling place. His personality is all over the new Jerusalem. We can tell what God is like simply by walking through His house.

Third, *this city calls us to glorify Jesus Christ.* As stated earlier, the existing heavens and earth were created to declare God's glory. Likewise, the new Heaven and earth will be so constructed as to manifest His glory most fully. To glorify God is the aim of all creation, both old and new, and that includes you and me.

The Westminster Catechism asks, "What is the chief end of man? The answer is, "To glorify God and to enjoy Him forever." Paul writes, "Whatever you do, do all to the glory of God" (1 Corinthians 10:31).

Because God will be so uniquely glorified in Heaven, let Him be glorified now in every aspect of your life.

HOME AT LAST!

A prominent citizen in town was dying, surrounded at his bedside by his family and physician.

As he thought of his massive wealth he had worked all

134

his life to amass, he whispered with a note of despair, "I'm *leaving* home, I'm *leaving* home."

Across town, a similar yet very different scene took place. There lay a solitary figure in meager, bare surroundings—a poor woman who had barely eked out a living for her children. Her modest home contained only the most basic of life's essentials. But in her heart dwelt the hope of Heaven.

Before she died, she was heard to say expectantly, "I'm *going* home, I'm *going* home."

What a different perspective for those who know God and who look to Heaven!

Is Heaven your home? The vast wealth and riches of the Eternal City is prepared for those who have made prior reservations through personal faith in God's Son, Jesus Christ. Put your faith in Him, and one day when you die— or when He returns—He will take you to your true home in Heaven.

In that day, we will discover it *just* doesn't get any better than this!

NOTES

1. J. Vernon McGee, *Revelation 14–22* (Nashville, TN: Thomas Nelson, 1991), pages 179-180.

2. John Phillips, *Exploring Revelation* (Neptune, NJ: Loizeaux Brothers, 1991), page 254

Chapter Eight

THE GREAT GETAWAY

The Escape of Heaven

Revelation 21:22-27

*A*S I WRITE THESE WORDS, I AM FLYING BACK home and have just pulled out the airline's magazine from the seat pocket in front of me. It's their publication that shows all the vacation getaways they offer.

On the front cover is an alluring picture of Disneyworld. There's Mickey and Minnie Mouse standing in front of the Magic Kingdom. Everyone's smiling and happy in the picture. Makes you want to get on a plane and go—preferably on one of their planes.

Inside are glamorous pictures of exciting vacation packages for people who desperately want to get away from it all. The enticing options are endless. Orlando. The Bahamas. Canada. Hawaii. Palm Springs. Paris. London. Miami.

The airline has definitely tapped into a major felt need—the desire for pressure-packed people to *get away* from the stresses and tensions of life. We live in such a fast-paced society that we need to get away from the crunch and daily grind to rest. We feel like a mummy—pressed for time—in need of escaping the heavy demands, problem people, pressing deadlines—the whole stinkin' mess.

But guess what?

You *can't* get away from it all—not and remain on this planet. No matter where you try to escape, you carry your baggage with you. You can pack your bag and go on a relaxing weekend trip, but you still fold up your stress in the same suitcase and carry it onto the plane with you. Before your plane can even land, your pressures are already at the

138

gate waiting for you to get off. You can run, but you can't hide. Truth is, we *can't* escape it all.

There's really only one place to go to escape your problems. Only one place to go to escape the crunch of life. Only one place to run and find relief.

That place, you ask?

Heaven.

Whatever it is that you long to escape, Heaven is the only place where you can escape it. Everybody's trying to get away. But only Heaven allows us the relief we so desperately need.

As we come to the concluding verses of Revelation 21, John is careful to describe for us what will *not* be in Heaven. That may sound negative, but it is intensely positive. Heaven will be Heaven as much for what will *not* be there as what *is* there. Having told us what and who will be there, the apostle will now tell us what and who will be *missing*.

Here are the *blessed absences* of heaven. There will be *no sanctuary* (verse 22), *no sun* (verse 23), *no self-glory* (verses 24-26), *no sin* (verse 27), and *no sinners* (verse 27).

NO SANCTUARY!

First, Heaven means that we will no longer be kept from seeing God, who has confined His presence since the Garden of Eden. In the new created order, there will be no sanctuary—no temple.

> *And I saw no temple in it, for the Lord God, the Almighty, and the Lamb, are its temple.* (Revelation 21:22)

Presently in Heaven, there is a temple containing the glory of God. Earlier in Revelation, John described this special inner chamber room: "The temple of God which is in heaven was opened, and the ark of His covenant appeared in His temple" (Revelation 11:19). The Holy of Holies was the innermost room in the Temple where the Ark of the Covenant resided. Here is the innermost room of Heaven—the throne room.

The Temple was the center of God's presence, the

primary place of worshiping God—the permanent abode of the Shekinah glory of God.

This temple in Heaven serves as the throne room of God where He administrates the affairs of this world. It is from this "Oval Office" that He dispatches the angels to carry out His executive orders. Earlier in the book of Revelation, John wrote further about this heavenly temple, "And another angel came out of the temple crying . . . 'Put in your sickle and reap, because the hour to reap has come. . . .' And another angel came out of the temple which is in heaven, and he also had a sharp sickle" (Revelation 14:15,17; see also 15:5-6; 16:17).

But now John observes that there is *no* heavenly temple! "For the Lord God, the Almighty, and the Lamb, are its temple" (verse 22). Why? Because God *Himself* is now the temple.

What is the significance of there being *no* temple?

Plenty!

No temple is needed in the new city because God's glory will be everywhere in full, visible.

In the eternal state, God Himself will dwell among His people in direct, immediate communion. In Heaven, God *is* the temple, meaning the entire city contains His immediate presence. God's glory is manifested *everywhere* in the new Jerusalem! Throughout all eternity, all citizens of the heavenly city will forever enjoy immediate access to God and unbroken fellowship with Jesus Christ.

Throughout history, God has sought to do one primary thing—to cause man to see, experience, and enjoy His glory. This began in the very beginning in the Garden of Eden. Adam and Eve lived in the presence of God, specifically with the Shekinah of God manifested as glorious light. But the first couple sinned and were cut off from God's glory (Genesis 3:24). From that point on, God has initiated different ways to get man to see His glory.

In the wilderness, Moses asked to see God's glory. "I pray Thee, show me Thy glory!" (Exodus 33:18). God replied, "I Myself will make all My goodness pass before you, and will proclaim the name of the LORD before you" (verse

19). So God caused His glory to pass before Moses while his servant hid in a rock. Why? Because no one can see the *full* glory of God and live. After seeing merely the afterglow of God's glory, Moses' face glowed like the noonday sun.

When the Israelites moved about in the wilderness, they were led by a great white cloud in the daytime and by a pillar of fire at night—the Shekinah glory of God (Exodus 13:21). When the Tabernacle was built, "the cloud covered the tent of meeting, and the glory of the LORD filled the tabernacle" (40:34). When the glory of God remained in the Tabernacle, the people were to camp there. But when the glory of God went into the sky as a cloud, or pillar of fire, the people were to move out.

After Israel had been in the Promised Land for a number of years, God instructed Solomon to build a temple (2 Samuel 7:12-13). When the Temple was built, "the cloud filled the house of the LORD, so that the priests could not stand to minister because of the cloud, for the glory of the LORD filled the house of the LORD" (1 Kings 8:10-11). God's glory now filled the Temple!

But when the Temple was turned into a place of idolatry, God's glory departed (Ezekiel 10:18-19, 11:22-23). Ichabod was written across the Temple door, meaning "the glory has departed" (1 Samuel 4:21). The glory of God was gone!

One more time God revealed His glory to man. When Jesus Christ became a man at His incarnation, He became the embodiment of the Shekinah. The disciple John wrote, "We beheld His glory . . . the glory of the only begotten from the Father" (John 1:14,18).

But Jesus was crucified and soon ascended to Heaven, to the right hand of God the Father (Acts 1:9-11) where God's glory now resides. When Christ returns, He will come "on the clouds of the sky with power and great glory" (Matthew 24:30). He will come back escorted by the Shekinah glory of God.

Until then, the glory of God is displayed in Christ's Body, the Church (Ephesians 3:19-21). In this present age,

God calls us to manifest His glory to a watching world (Colossians 1:27).

At the present time, God's glory is now fully displayed around His throne in Heaven. As Christ is enthroned at God's right hand, the throne room—or the heavenly Temple—is that place of greatest glory.

When Stephen was martyred, "he gazed intently into heaven and saw the glory of God, and Jesus standing at the right hand of God" (Acts 7:55). That's where God's Shekinah glory resides now—in Heaven, in God's presence, in the Temple in Heaven, where Christ is seated.

Over the course of time, God's glory has been displayed in various ways. He revealed His glory in the Garden (Adam and Eve), the face of a man (Moses), in the sky (cloud and pillar of fire), in a tent (tabernacle), in a building (temple), in Christ, and in the Church (believers). But most of all, it is revealed in Heaven in the heavenly Temple (throne room).

So, let me ask the question again: What is the significance of John's statement, "I saw no temple" (Revelation 21:22)?

This passage means that in the new Heaven, there will be no localized, consolidated, designated dwelling place for the glory of God. Instead, God's glory will fill and permeate the *entire* new Heaven—not just one centralized place. Thus, wherever we go in Heaven, we will be in the immediate presence of the full glory of God. Wherever we go, we will enjoy the complete manifestation of God's presence. Throughout all eternity, we will *never* be separated from direct, unhindered fellowship with God.

NO SUN!

Second, because there will be no sanctuary, there will be no sun. This is a cause and effect. The former produces the latter.

> *And the city has no need of the sun or of moon to shine upon it, for the glory of God has illumined it, and its lamp is the Lamb.* (Revelation 21:23)

There will be no sun in the eternal, celestial city because the glory of God will be the source of all uncreated light. His glory is so bright, there will be no need of any artificial light.

The sun and moon will be snuffed out, never to shine again. Their services will not be needed in the eternal city.

The sun is a huge, glowing ball of gases at the center of the solar system. A yellow dwarf star, it has an average surface temperature of about 5,800 K (10,000°F). Now, that's only the *cool* season! Temperatures can shoot up to 1,000,000 K (1,800,000°F) when the weather really heats up. The outer atmosphere of the sun has a temperature of about 2,000,000 K (3,600,000°F).

The visible surface consists of hot gases that give off light and heat. So much energy is given off, in fact, that only about a two-billionth of the sun's light and heat reaches the earth. The rest is lost in space.

All life on the earth—people, animals, and plants—depends on the energy from the sun. Plants use sunlight to make their own food and, in the process, give off oxygen. People and animals eat the plants and breathe in the oxygen. In turn, we breathe out carbon dioxide, which plants combine with energy from sunlight and water from the soil to produce more food.

The temperature of any particular place on the earth depends on its proximity to the sun. Tropical regions near the equator have a hot climate because the sun shines almost directly overhead at noon. Arctic regions near the North and South Poles have a cold climate because the sun never rises above the horizon.

Now—and this is incredible—God will snuff out the sun! This huge, blazing star will be extinguished by the Lord, the way we would blow out a birthday candle. *Whssssssh!* And the sun will cease to shine—forever!

While the sun was once the source of life for all on the earth, God Himself will then be our energy source. All life in the new Heaven—whether human, animal, or plant life—will be dependent upon the effulgent light of the glory of God for its life!

The sun and moon of the first creation (Genesis 1:14-16)

will have no place in the new creation to come (Revelation 21:1). "The moon will be abashed and the sun ashamed" (Isaiah 24:23). The new creation will be lighted by the Shekinah glory of God.

The light that blazed from the face of Jesus on the Mount of Transfiguration (Matthew 17:1-4) will be the sole illumination in the heavenly Jerusalem. We will walk in the light of His countenance.

Consequently, there will be no night, no darkness, and no shadows in the eternal state—only one bright, constant daytime. "And there shall no longer be any night; and they shall not have need of the light of a lamp nor the light of the sun, because the Lord God shall illumine them" (Revelation 22:5).

Throughout the Bible, darkness represents evil and ignorance of the knowledge of God. But light pictures holiness and the personal knowledge of God. Because there will be only the light of God's glory in the new Heaven, this pictures that the full knowledge of God will be ours in His presence.

NO SELF-GLORY!

Third, there will be no self-glory in Heaven. It is the place where Christ alone is in the place of preeminence. He alone will be worshiped.

> *And the nations shall walk by its light, and the kings of the earth shall bring their glory into it. And in the daytime (for there shall be no night there) its gates shall never be closed; and they shall bring the glory and the honor of the nations into it.* (Revelation 21:24-26)

A remnant of the nations, once pagan and rebellious, now also are in Heaven, since they were converted by the gospel during their days on earth. "The kings of the earth" represent the nations that they once led and governed. All these believing saints now come into the new Jerusalem to worship God and give Him glory. These kings, who had once been the objects of homage upon the earth, now give

144

their homage to Christ. Even the mightiest men of earth will bow before His throne.

The kings will acknowledge that Christ rules over all. Their faces will turn upward and give glory and honor to Him who sits upon the throne. These one-time representatives of all the earth's peoples will lead their former subjects in worshiping Christ.

At Christ's birth, the magi—the mighty king makers of the East—came to the Holy Child, led by the light of God's glory, and gave their glory and honor to Him.

> *The star [austere, bright light of God's glory], which they had seen in the east, went on before them, until it came and stood over where the Child was. And when they saw the star, they rejoiced exceedingly with great joy. And they came into the house and saw the Child with Mary His mother; and they fell down and worshiped Him; and opening their treasures they presented to Him gifts of gold and frankincense and myrrh.* (Matthew 2:9-11)

The worship of the magi will be repeated over and over and over throughout all eternity. The one time mighty kings of the earth and all the converted nations with them will bring their glory, honor, and treasures into the holy city to offer their worship to Christ.

The glory of the nations and kings is a derived glory, received from Christ Himself. They come into the Holy City in order to lay their honor down at His feet. They will bring their worship and praise to God as a part of the blood-washed throng, thus fulfilling the very purpose for which they were created. All the nations will walk in the light of God's presence.

Because the gates of the new Jerusalem will never be closed, there will be no shutting out worshipers from bringing their praises to God! The open gates suggest unhindered communication between God and man, between Heaven and earth, between the Creator and His creation. There will be a continual parade of glorified saints proceeding into the new Jerusalem throughout all eternity. Because there will be no sun and no night, its gates will never be closed. Thus, worship will occur around the clock—even in the wee hours of the morning.

In ancient days, the city gates were closed at night for protection against thieves, enemies, and wild animals. But these pearly gates need never be closed because there is no night and no thieves. They are always open because there is no need for protection from harm.

John MacArthur writes, "Perfect praise will be the highest, noblest expression of our perfected being. We will recognize the splendor of God. We will see clearly His glory and perfection. And gazing on God's perfections eternally will compel us to offer uninterrupted, unrestrained, adoring, loving worship—it will be our delight!"[1]

NO SIN!
Heaven will be environmentally safe from the pollution of sin.

> *And nothing unclean . . . shall ever come into it.*
> (Revelation 21:27)

All the major cities of the earth today are great centers of sin. Our cities have become the melting pots of gang violence, mob activity, and all forms of sinful life. But not this city! Nothing unclean will ever come into it—*nothing!*

"Nothing unclean" refers to all sinful practices. There will not be even the slightest trace of sin in Heaven.

First, *there will be nothing unclean within us.* In our glorified state, we will be fully conformed to the image of Christ. All indwelling sin will be completely eradicated. Our sinful flesh will be removed and we will be made perfect. We will finally live without any sinful thoughts, selfish motives, or wrong actions. Scripture calls this final state glorification (Romans 8:30).

Glorification is the final stage of salvation in which all believers will be presented to God with the last evidences of indwelling sin destroyed. We will be made perfect and complete, and only then will we fully reflect the glory of our

146

Creator. The positional righteousness we received in justification the day we were born again will now be completed within us. Thus, glorification is the practical finish to justification.

Each aspect of our inner man will function in divine righteousness. Our minds will intimately and clearly know God, submit to God, and understand divine truth. Our hearts will love God with a singular affection. Our volition will spontaneously choose obedience to God. Our consciences will be free from all guilt and will desire and approve only righteous, moral decisions. Our souls and spirits will assimilate all the aspects of our inner man with our glorified bodies to serve God best. Thus, the removal of the sin nature will give us unrestricted freedom to function as God originally designed and created us.

Originally, man was free to choose and participate in good or evil. However, it was not necessary for him to sin. The Fall defiled man's capacity for righteousness as he became a slave to sin. From that point on even his good choices were tainted with sin. Redeemed man received a new nature and has two capacities. He possesses a freedom and preference to serve righteousness, yet may exercise his Adamic nature to sin. He can sin, but need not. Glorified man has only the divine capacity to serve righteousness because his sinful flesh will be eradicated.

In Heaven, we will become holy as Christ is holy. Christ serves as an excellent example of what will be our glorified nature. Christ's impeccability teaches that because Christ was holy, He was not able to sin. Clearly Christ was tempted to sin (Matthew 4:1-11), but because He had no sin nature He was not susceptible to sin.[2] He had only the capacity for divine holiness. That's the way it will be when we are made like Christ in glorification. We will be made holy. Consequently, we will not have the capacity to sin.

"We shall be like Him, because we shall see Him just as He is" (1 John 3:2).

Gutzon Borglum, the sculptor, was once carving a statue of a head. A woman who regularly swept out his studio wondered who he was sculpting.

One day she finally recognized who the image was. It was obvious now. The master sculptor was carving the face of President Abraham Lincoln in marble.

Very much surprised, she turned to Borglum and inquired, "How did you know that Mr. Lincoln was in that piece of stone?"

To which he responded, "That's simple. I just chisel away everything that doesn't look like the president."

That's what God is doing in our lives—carving us into the image of Jesus Christ. Today our likeness to Christ may not be as close as we would like it to be. But one day, in Heaven, when we step into His presence, all sin will be chiseled away from us—resulting in perfect Christlikeness. We will be made fully in His image.

Can you imagine yourself looking like that?

This is what John meant when he wrote, "Beloved, now we are children of God, and it has not appeared as yet what we shall be. We know that, when He appears, we shall be like Him, because we shall see Him just as He is" (1 John 3:2).

Second, *there will be nothing unclean around us.* We will live in a world spiritually clean from the pollution of all sin.

In the new Jerusalem, there will be *no* funeral homes, *no* hospitals, *no* abortion clinics, *no* divorce courts, *no* brothels, *no* bankruptcy courts, *no* psychiatric wards, and *no* treatment centers.

There will be *no* pornography, *no* dial-a-porn, *no* teen suicide, *no* AIDS, *no* cancer, *no* talk shows, *no* rape, *no* missing children, *no* gay rights marches, *no* drug problems, *no* drive-by shootings, *no* racial tension, and *no* prejudice.

There will be *no* misunderstandings, *no* injustice, *no* depression, *no* hurtful words, *no* gossip, *no* hurt feelings, *no* worry, *no* emptiness, and *no* child abuse.

There will be *no* wars, *no* financial worries, *no* emotional heartaches, *no* physical pain, *no* spiritual flatness, *no* relational divisions, *no* murders, and *no* casseroles.

There will be *no* tears, *no* suffering, *no* separations, no starvation, *no* arguments, *no* accidents, *no* emergency departments, *no* doctors, *no* nurses, *no* heart monitors, *no* rust, *no* perplexing questions, *no* false teachers, *no* financial shortages, *no* hurricanes, *no* bad habits, *no* decay, and *no* locks.

We will never need to confess sin. Never need to apologize again. Never need to straighten out a strained relationship. Never have to resist Satan again. Never have to resist temptation.

Never!

NO SINNERS!

Finally, *no sinners* will be admitted into Heaven. Not just no sin, but no sinners will be allowed to enter into God's presence.

> *No one who practices abomination and lying, shall ever come into it, but only those whose names are written in the Lamb's book of life.* (Revelation 21:27)

Anyone whose lifestyle on earth consisted of "abominations and lying" will never enter Heaven. This refers to those who constantly practice these evils. It describes the direction and pattern of one's life, not merely isolated acts of sin, and reveals that they were never converted.

Abomination refers to all types of sinful perversions—literally, pollution. Thus, no polluted mouth will be admitted. No polluted mind will enter. No polluted hands will be permitted. Instead, "for the . . . abominable . . . their part will be in the lake that burns with fire and brimstone, which is the second death" (21:8).

Lying refers to unbelievers who spread false teaching and bear false witness. Only those whose names are written in the Lamb's book of life will enter into the celestial city. Only those who have placed saving faith in Jesus Christ and undergone a radical transformation of heart and life. God's transforming grace causes us to speak with truth in our new daily walk. All the Bible supports this exclusivity. No sinners will enter the kingdom of Heaven! Paul wrote, "Or do you not know that the unrighteous shall not inherit the kingdom of God? Do not be deceived; neither fornicators, nor idolaters, nor adulterers, nor effeminate, nor homosexuals, nor thieves, nor the covetous, nor drunkards, nor revilers, nor swindlers, shall inherit the kingdom of God" (1 Corinthians 6:9-10).

Paul clarifies that those who practice the deeds of the flesh are unconverted and will never enter Heaven. Here is the lifestyle of those who will be excluded from God's presence forever.

Now the deeds of the flesh are evident, which are: immorality, impurity, sensuality, idolatry, sorcery, enmities, strife, jealousy, outbursts of anger, disputes, dissensions, factions, envying, drunkenness, carousing, and things like these, of which I forewarn you just as I forewarned you that those who practice such things shall not inherit the kingdom of God. (Galatians 5:19-21)

Lest there be any doubt in our minds, Paul speaks emphatically and categorically, "For this you know with certainty, that no immoral or impure person or covetous man, who is an idolater, has an inheritance in the kingdom of Christ and God" (Ephesians 5:5).

Heaven is an exclusive place!

It's not for everyone!

The Bible says there are many dwelling places in Heaven, but relatively few make it there. Jesus warned, "The gate is wide, and the way is broad that leads to destruction, and many are those who enter by it. For the gate is small, and the way is narrow that leads to life, and few are those who find it" (Matthew 7:13-14).

Heaven belongs only to those, John says, whose names are written in the Lamb's book of life. Its citizens are those who have repented of their sins and believed upon Christ in their hearts. The Lamb's book of life is Heaven's register of everyone who has believed in Christ with saving faith. They alone will enter its gates. "Blessed are those who wash their robes, that they may have the right to . . . enter by the gates into the city" (Revelation 22:14).

Do you know Christ personally?

Are you Heaven bound?

THE ESCAPE THAT SAVES

One evening a woman was driving home when she noticed a huge truck behind her that was driving uncomfortably close. The headlights were shining in her rearview mirror, blinding her eyes.

She stepped on the gas to put some distance between her and the truck—but to no avail. When she sped up, the truck sped up. The faster she drove, the faster the truck followed.

Her heart began to pound. With sweaty palms, she turned the steering wheel and took the next exit ramp off the freeway. But the truck stayed with her as closely as ever. Now frantic, this woman turned up a main street, hoping to lose her stalking pursuer in the traffic. But the truck ran a red light and continued to chase her.

Reaching the panic point, the woman whipped her car into a service station, threw open the door, and bolted across the pavement screaming for help.

The truck driver jumped from his rig and ran toward her. He yanked open her back door and pulled out a man who was hidden in her back seat.

The woman had been running from the wrong person!

Unknown to her, the truck driver had spotted a would-be rapist in the back seat of her car. The chase was not his effort to harm her. His pursuit was intended to save her, even at the cost of his own safety.

His desire was to help the woman escape that which would harm her.

Many people are like that woman. They run from God, fearing what He might do to them. But if they would only stop running from God, He would give them their escape from what truly threatens to harm them—Satan, sin, and the second death.

Heaven is the great escape. Only there in Heaven will we escape sin because we will be glorified. We will escape disease because we will receive perfected bodies. We will escape stress because we will receive God's rest. We will escape conflict because we will receive God's peace. We will escape boredom because we will worship the thrice holy

Sovereign of Heaven. We will escape loneliness because we will have come "to the general assembly and church of the first-born" (Hebrews 12:23). We will escape insignificance because we will fully realize our true identity in Christ. We will escape death because we have put off the perishable and put on the imperishable.

Heaven, the dwelling place of God, is a perfect place where we will escape every conceivable imperfection.

Heaven, indeed, is the Great Getaway.

Everyone is trying to get away from it all.

But only Heaven delivers.

NOTES
1. John MacArthur, *Heaven* (Panorama City, CA: Word of Grace Publications, 1988), page 101.
2. For an in-depth look at Christ's impeccability, see John F. Walvoord, *Jesus Christ Our Lord* (Chicago: Moody Press, 1969) pp. 145-152. Also see Steven J Lawson, *Faith Under Fire*, ch. 11 (Wheaton, IL: Crossway Publishers, 1995).

Chapter Nine

FROM HERE TO ETERNITY

The Glory of Heaven

Revelation 22:1-5

⟨ENTURIES AGO, ANCIENT MARINERS SAILED THE *Mediterranean Sea, hugging the familiar coastline, follow-ing the chartered shores, never letting land out of sight.

As they sailed westward, they were eventually con-fronted with a difficult decision. That dilemma was the Strait of Gibraltar. The Pillars of Hercules. The famous pas-sage leading out into the vast Atlantic.

On this side of those towering boulders was the Mediterranean Sea, chartered territory, known worlds, dis-covered lands.

But beyond lay the Atlantic Ocean—the unknown, the unexplored, the undiscovered, and the seemingly unend-ing. It was one thing for these sailors to navigate the Mediterranean with land in full view. But it was something else entirely to venture through Gibraltar into the great Atlantic and sail into the endless horizon with no land in sight.

As the frail ships passed through the Straits—the mas-sive Pillars of Hercules—the ancient mariners would say, "*Ne plus uttra,*" which means, "There is nothing beyond!"

With this passage, the mariners were leaving the known world of the coastline and sailing into a vast, undiscovered world of the open sea.

That's what the Apostle John is saying to us now—"*Ne plus uttra.*" There is nothing beyond this description of the new Jerusalem but worlds unknown! With these last verses of the book of Revelation, we are sailing out into the unknown world of eternity with no end in sight. We leave the shoreline of time and launch out into eternity future—with all its vastness and immensity.

We have been touring the new Jerusalem, beginning with Revelation 21. We have seen, first, the *descent* of the city like a bride adorned (21:1-8); second, the *dimensions* of the city—1,500 miles wide, long, and high (21:9-17); the *material* of the city—with costly stones, gates of pearl, walls of diamonds, streets of gold (21:18-21); and fourth, the *perfection* of the city (22:1-5), a beautiful garden—Paradise—reminiscent of the Garden of Eden.

These verses reflect the Paradise-like qualities of the new Jerusalem and bring the message of the Bible to completion. Paradise lost in Adam (Genesis 3) is now Paradise regained in Christ (Revelation 21–22).

Everything is now made perfect. Heaven is a *perfect* place, created by a *perfect* God, indwelt by *perfect* people, who offer *perfect* worship to Him. Heaven is the most perfect place we'll ever experience.

A RIVER RUNS THROUGH IT

First, John describes the river of life that was promised earlier to the one who thirsts (Revelation 21:6). From this stream, which flows through Heaven, we will be fully satisfied, fulfilled, and blessed!

> *And he showed me a river of the water of life, clear as crystal, coming from the throne of God and of the Lamb, in the middle of its street. (Revelation 22:1-2)*

Here is a crystal-clear stream gushing out of God's throne—remember, there is only one throne occupied by both God and Christ (Revelation 3:21)—and flowing down the middle of the street of gold—the central thoroughfare in Heaven where everyone travels. I believe this is a *literal* river flowing through a *literal* city occupied by *literal* people in a *literal* place called Heaven.

When the heavenly citizens drink from this life-giving stream, it brings exhilarating ecstasy. The psalmist boasts,

"There is a river whose streams make glad the city of God" (Psalm 46:4). This river of life is accessible to all!

Such joy was available at the dawn of human history. In Eden, a beautiful river flowed in the garden and divided into four streams, proving enrichment for all who drank. But the entrance of sin into the world soon dammed up its flow (Genesis 2:6,10). In Heaven, this river of life will flow again, bringing God's eternal blessing to His people.

This river shimmers as it reflects the glory of God. This is no muddy stream, polluted and contaminated by man's environmental abuses. It is crystal-clear and perfectly clean because it comes bubbling out of God's throne. The source of this stream is supernatural—a geyser of grace flowing from God and His Son to all Heaven's citizens.

Though a literal river, it is not without symbolic meaning. Here is a real river representing the inexhaustible grace of God forever flowing into our lives in Heaven. Here is the fullness of God's undiminished goodness, unlimited blessings, and His unfathomable provisions pouring into our lives and flooding our hearts.

In ancient Palestine, a river was always a welcome place of comfort, rest, refreshment, and sustenance. It meant cool water to dry mouths parched by the arid desert. Imagine the joy of a weary traveler in the hot wilderness who came upon a crystal-clear, cool river! That will be our constant delight in Heaven after years of weary traveling in this wilderness of sin. Our tired bodies and burdened souls will be refreshed to the fullest.

Jesus Himself will lead us to this river to drink. "The Lamb . . . shall guide them to springs of the water of life" (Revelation 7:17). We will drink as much as we want, as long as we want. Our bodies will find strength, our souls will find satisfaction, and our spirits will find fulfillment forever. In this river is the quenching of all our hearts' desires, the slaking of all our thirsts.

GOD'S HEALTH CARE REFORM

On the two banks of the river of life grow many rows of the tree of life. John wrote:

> *And on either side of the river was the tree of life, bearing*
> *twelve kinds of fruit, yielding its fruit every month; and*
> *the leaves of the tree were for the healing of the nations.*
> (Revelation 22:2)

This "tree of life" designated in singular form, is probably a collective word meaning *many* trees of life. For how could one tree be on both sides of the river? Here are numerous trees—an entire *forest* perhaps—outlining the banks of the river of life.

William Hendrickson comments, "The idea is not that there is just one single tree. No, there is an entire park: whole rows of trees alongside the river between the river and the avenue. This is true with respect to all the avenues of the city."[1]

These trees yield an abundant supply of fruit of all different kinds—twelve in all. In Heaven, growing seasons for fruit will be a thing of the past, belonging to the old creation. Here will be a continuous bumper harvest, always yielding its produce.

When this fruit is eaten, it will produce *healing* (the Greek word is *therappein*, from which we get the English word *therapeutic),* meaning health-giving. Here is real "health food"! It perpetuates the vitality of this city's citizens and renews their physical and spiritual stamina.

This healing does not mean there will be illness in the new Jerusalem. There will be no disease because there will be no sin. Rather, it means that the tree of life will produce all sorts of blessedness—vitality, fulfillment, satisfaction, strength, renewal, and well-being.

In the Garden of Eden, the tree of life represented perpetual physical life. But when man sinned, he was driven away from the tree of life and death entered the human race. Sickness, sorrow, and weakness resulted. Now, access to the tree of life is restored. Man will live forever in God's presence, enjoying the fullness of His favor.

This is the promise Christ makes to all believers. "To him who overcomes, I will grant to eat of the tree of life, which is in the Paradise of God" (Revelation 2:7). The multifaceted blessing of God will be ours in the garden of Heaven when we eat and enjoy this fruit.

Will we literally eat and drink in Heaven?

Absolutely!

Jesus said, "I will not drink of the fruit of the vine from now on until the kingdom of God comes" (Luke 22:18). In Heaven, we will participate in the marriage supper of the Lamb. A supper implies that we will have a feast together!

A Philadelphia law firm sent flowers to an associate in Baltimore upon the opening of its new offices. Through some mix-up, the ribbon that bedecked the floral piece read "Deepest Sympathy."

When the florist was informed of his mistake, he let out a cry of alarm. "Good heavens," he exclaimed, "then the flowers that went to the funeral said, 'Congratulations on your new location!'"

Heaven *will be* a wonderful new location.

CURSE THE CURSE!

We will be free from the contamination of any sin!

> *And there shall no longer be any curse.* (Revelation 22:3)

At long last, God's curse upon creation will be removed— the curse pronounced upon all mankind because of Adam's sin, which has subjected all creation to futility (Genesis 3:14-19). The earth bears the ugly scars of sin—pollution, droughts, erosion, floods, fires, thorns, and thistles. But the new creation will be delivered from this curse.

First, the animals and Satan have been cursed. Enmity, or a hostile separation, has been placed between animals.

> *And the LORD God said to the serpent,*
> *"Because you have done this,*
> *Cursed are you more than all cattle,*
> *And more than every beast of the field;*
> *On your belly shall you go,*
> *And dust shall you eat*
> *All the days of your life;*

And I will put enmity
Between you and the woman,
And between your seed and her seed;
He shall bruise you on the head,
And you shall bruise him on the heel." (Genesis 3:14-15)

Second, women have been cursed.

To the woman, He said,
"I will greatly multiply
Your pain in childbirth;
In pain you shall bring forth children;
Yet your desire shall be for your husband,
And he shall rule over you." (Genesis 3:16)

In this judgment, women experience pain in childbearing and desire to dominate their husbands—a source of immeasurable sorrow.

Third, men and the earth have been judged by God.

Then to Adam He said, "Because you have listened
to the voice of your wife, and have eaten from the tree
about which I commanded you, saying, 'You shall not
    eat from it';
"Cursed is the ground because of you;
In toil you shall eat of it
All the days of your life.
Both thorns and thistles, it shall grow for you;
And you shall eat the plants of the field;
By the sweat of your face
You shall eat bread,
Till you return to the ground,
Because from it you were taken;
For you are dust,
And to dust you shall return." (Genesis 3:17-19)

The cursed earth will produce thorns and thistles. Growing food will become a chore. Work will be accompanied by pain and weariness. Life will end with death.

But in the new creation, the curse is removed! God will reverse the effects of sin in the heavenly city. "There will be no more curse, for Jerusalem will dwell in security" (Zechariah 14:11).

Heaven will be free from the effects of all sin. No more contending with Satan. No more pain and sorrow. No more death and separation. No more ruthless tyranny by godless men. No more hostility. No more disease and illness. Only peace and health, comfort and pleasure.

We have never known one moment like this—but we will one day. In Heaven we will finally come out from under the staggering effects of Adam's original sin. We will be completely immersed in the powerful effect of Christ's obedience at the cross.

THERE'S REIGN IN THE FORECAST

Heaven will be governed, not by a democracy, monarchy, oligarchy, or diocracy, but by a theocracy—the government of God. In Heaven, the throne of God the Father and Christ will be in the midst of it, signifying the completeness and universality of God's reign.

And the throne of God and of the Lamb shall be in it.
(Revelation 22:3)

God's throne is that seat of unrivaled, universal sovereignty. It is the headquarters of all creation. The place of executive dominion, jointly held together by the Father and the Son. They will reign without any competition. No more will Satan, demons, evil men, tyrants, dictators, or self-serving politicians dominate the nations. God and Jesus Christ alone will rule!

This Kingdom will be forever! "The LORD sits as King forever" (Psalm 29:10). The angels announced, "He [Christ] will reign over the house of Jacob forever; and His kingdom will have no end" (Luke 1:33). God's reign will be unending, unhindered, and unrivaled.

Paul writes, "[God] seated Him at His right hand in the heavenly places far above all rule and authority and power

160

and dominion, and every name that is named, not only in this age, but also in the one to come" (Ephesians 1:20-21). In the age to come—eternity future—the reign of Christ will be over all.

IN HIS MAJESTY'S SERVICE

Heaven will provide limitless opportunities to serve God. In eternity, we will have meaningful ministry assignments to perform. John writes:

And His bond-servants shall serve Him. (Revelation 22:3)

The apostle uses the future tense meaning we "shall keep on serving Him forever and ever." *Serve (lutreo)* refers to the priestly service offered to God. Earlier in Revelation, John wrote that God has made us to be a kingdom of priests (Revelation 1:6), and what do priests do but serve God?

God has built into our human nature a creative drive to accomplish something meaningful and productive. There is a noble ambition within us to meet worthy goals and achieve notable objectives. Rightfully so, we derive pleasure from a job well done (Ecclesiastes 3:24). This God-given, creative drive will be no less a part of our glorified humanity in Heaven. In fact, this holy ambition will be intensified and elevated to new heights. Because our sin nature will be eradicated, we will serve God with a pure heart.

In eternity, we will fully know the joy of accomplishing something great for God. We will know the thrill of performing God-given tasks perfectly. We will have glorified bodies, sinless hearts, and perfect skills with which to serve Him. We will never grow tired or mess up our assigned responsibilities.

In Heaven, we will be busier than ever. We will be engaged in ceaseless activity since there is no night. Actually, the more we serve God in Heaven, the more refreshed we will be. Like the disciples who had more fish and bread left over after feeding the five thousand, the Lord will multiply our efforts exponentially. We will serve Him continuously yet never become exhausted. There will be no burn-out in

Heaven. No mid-life crisis. No retirement. We will only feel replenished and invigorated.

W. A. Criswell, the famous pastor of First Baptist Church in Dallas, Texas, once said, "I long to preach in heaven, there will be no clocks there." As a preacher, I can relate to that—no noon deadlines. We will just serve God forever and never feel any restraints.

Who knows? God may give each of us our own solar system or a galaxy to operate. After all, Adam was given dominion over the old creation on this earth.

I CAN SEE CLEARLY NOW, THE REIGN IS COME!

Heaven will be a place in which we will see the greatest of all sights—Jesus Christ! We will behold Him face-to-face, up close, in person, with our very own eyes! John writes:

And they shall see His face. (Revelation 22:4)

This divine vision is the supreme blessedness of Heaven. It describes what the theologians call "the beatific vision." This is the sight of God that will provoke instant and profound joy. It is the ultimate blessedness for which every one of us was created.

In Heaven, we will actually see the glorified Christ! Presently we walk by faith, and God is veiled to our mortal eyes. Peter writes, "Though you have not seen Him, you love Him, and though you do not see Him now, but believe in Him, you greatly rejoice with joy inexpressible and full of glory" (1 Peter 1:8).

R. C. Sproul has said, "There is no more difficult problem that attends the life of faith than that we are called to serve and worship God who is utterly invisible to us. As long as we are tainted by sin, we cannot see God. Presently, we cannot look upon a holy God and live. "[2]

God is now invisible to all mortals. All Scripture testifies to this. God declared to Moses, "No man can see Me and live!" (Exodus 33:20). Paul writes, "[God] alone possesses immortality and dwells in unapproachable light; whom no man has seen or can see" (1 Timothy 6:16). Likewise, John penned, "No one has beheld God at any time" (1 John 4:12).

However, in Heaven, we will see our God!

In that split second when we enter into His presence, we will be glorified and then see Him in His glory. This was certainly Job's hope who said, "Even after my skin is destroyed, yet from my flesh I shall see God; Whom I myself shall behold, and Whom my eyes shall see and not another. My heart faints within me" (Job 19:26-27). This pain-ridden patriarch confidently said that after death he would see God in a glorified, resurrection body.

This was certainly the psalmist's hope. David wrote, "As for me, I shall behold Thy face in righteousness; I will be satisfied with Thy likeness when I awake" (Psalm 17:15).

Jesus promised, "Blessed are the pure in heart, for they shall see God" (Matthew 5:8). In Heaven, we will be made absolutely pure in heart, and we will finally see God perfectly. As in a mirror dimly, we now see God through the eyes of faith. But then we will look directly into the face of Christ (1 Corinthians 13:12).

Even in Heaven, though, we will not see God in His totality. He is infinite and we, even though glorified, will still be finite humanity. There is no way for finite man to fully comprehend an infinite God.

Specifically, what will we see? God is Spirit—He has no body parts. As an incorporeal Being, God will manifest His glory to us as bright light. In Heaven, we will see the bright, shining light of God's glory with our physical eyes.

In His presence, we will also more fully comprehend who He is. John MacArthur says, "Seeing God implies a far greater spiritual comprehension of God. We will see God with the eye of the mind. We will have an instantaneous awareness and knowledge of the fullness of God—as much as human beings have capacity for."[3] In other words, we will see God with glorified eyes. We will know God with perfected minds.

In ancient times, criminals were banished from the presence of the king. Likewise, Oriental kings secluded themselves from their own loyal subjects. To have an audience with an ancient king was a rare privilege—even for the highest ranked citizens. But in Heaven, we will be afforded an audience with the King! We will see Him—personally, intimately, directly, forever!

We will see Christ "just as He is" (1 John 3:2). We will look upon Him and clearly see His glory! Not as He *was*— humiliated on the cross, an obscure Galilean, a common carpenter, a suffering servant. Rather, we will see Him as He *is*—glorified at the Father's right hand, enthroned, in sovereignty, ruling in majesty. No aspect of His glory will be veiled. We will see "the blessed and only Sovereign, the King of kings and Lord of lords" (1 Timothy 6:15).

Seeing God and Christ will overwhelm us and thrill our enraptured souls forever.

GET THIS INTO YOUR HEAD!

Once in Heaven, Christ's name will be branded into our foreheads when we are glorified.

And His name shall be on their foreheads. (Revelation 22:4)

Christ's name refers to the character of God, or to the likeness of God. In the Bible, a name represents all that a person is. And it is also proof of one's ownership placed upon an object. In Heaven, His name will be inscribed on us. Therefore, we will be made completely like Him—body, soul, and spirit—and, thus, completely owned by Christ whose likeness we will uniquely bear. Each of us will be like Him, yet without disturbing our own individual identity or peculiar personality.

None of us will be lost in the anonymity of the crowd. We will be individually known to God and to one another. The citizens of the new Jerusalem will reflect and bear the glory of Christ.

Two Texans were trying to impress each other with the size of their ranches. One asked the other, "What's the name of your ranch?"

The rancher replied, "The Rocking R, ABC, Flying W,

Circle C, Bar, Stable Four, Box D, Rolling M, Rainbow's End, Silver Spur Ranch."

The first Texan was impressed and exclaimed, "Whew! That's sure some name! How many head of cattle do you run?"

The rancher answered, "Not many. Very few survive the branding."

Well, we will all survive this branding with Christ's name in Heaven! His name will be on our foreheads, meaning we will be like Him.

Looking ahead to this day, John writes, "Beloved, now we are children of God, and it has not appeared as yet what we shall be. We know that, when He appears, we shall be like Him" (1 John 3:2). We don't have all the details, but if we're going to be made like Christ, that's good enough for me. It couldn't be any better than that!

This means, first, a glorified body. Our physical bodies will be made like Christ's resurrection body. "The Lord Jesus Christ . . . will transform the body of our humble state into conformity with the body of His glory, by the exertion of the power that He has even to subject all things to Himself" (Philippians 3:20-21). We will have heavenly bodies that will be adapted to our new environment (1 Corinthians 15:35-49).

Likewise, we will have a glorified soul without any trace of our human fallenness. Our sin nature will be eradicated. The old man will be fully and forever put away—like a snake shedding its old skin. We will be instantly and completely perfected in our inner man. Glorified bodies will house "the spirits of righteous men made perfect" (Hebrews 12:23). In that day, the entire inner man—mind, emotion, and will—will be perfect, without any taint of sin.

This is the state of glorification. Paul spoke of it: "Whom He predestined, these He also called; and whom He called, these He also justified; and whom He justified, these He also glorified" (Romans 8:30). Glorified means we bear the glory of Christ. We will have perfect freedom from evil forever. We will never have a selfish thought. Never utter a useless word. Never perform an unkind deed.

Never again.

LET THE *SON* SHINE IN!

In addition, Heaven is a place of bright, blazing light emanating from God's splendid glory. His glory will illumine the universe with a dazzling display of divine light. John writes:

> *And there shall no longer be any night; and they shall not have need of the light of a lamp nor the light of the sun, because the Lord God shall illumine them.* (Revelation 22:5)

There will be no night there, as we have already discussed, because there will be no sun. There will be no more division of day and night. Eternity will be the dawning of a new day that will never die. We will have no need for lights, lamps, flashlights, or streetlights. No headlights, overhead lights, or floodlights.

God will snuff out the sun! The glory of God and Christ will light up the universe. "And the city has no need of the sun or the moon to shine upon it, for the glory of God has illumined it, and its lamp is the Lamb" (21:23).

The Shekinah glory of God will be constantly displayed before our very eyes. We will never lose sight of His majesty. Every moment of every day, forever and ever, the glorious light of Christ's presence will shine into our hearts and fill us with the fullness of His regal majesty.

WHO'LL STOP THE REIGN?

Finally, not only will we be servants in Heaven, but we will also be—and I say this reverently—kings. We will reign forever as kings over the new heavens and new earth. Not only will God reign, but we will reign with Him.

> *And they shall reign forever and ever. (Revelation 22:5)*

Who is "they" (plural) who reigns forever? It is a joint reign between God, the Lamb, and His bondservants. As glorified saints, we will reign eternally with God and Christ, world without end. God's people will reign under God, with God, and for God.

Here is the eventual fulfillment of the cultural mandate

that man should rule over God's creation. In the beginning, at the dawn of creation, God said, "Let us make man in Our image according to Our likeness; and let them rule over the fish of the sea and over the birds of the sky and over the cattle and over all the earth, and over every creeping thing that creeps on the earth . . . and subdue it" (Genesis 1:26,28). Even after Adam's sin, the mandate remained the same. David declared, "Thou dost make him [man] to rule over the works of Thy hands" (Psalm 8:6).

With this final truth, the message of the Bible has now come full circle. Dramatically, the message of the Bible is now complete!

What began in Genesis is now completed in Revelation. Genesis tells us how it all began; Revelation tells us how it all ends. All that lies between is the unfolding plan of redemption.

In Genesis we see the first Paradise closed. In Revelation we see the new Paradise opened. In Genesis we find the entrance of human sin. In Revelation we see the exclusion of human sin. In Genesis the curse was imposed. In Revelation the curse is removed. In Genesis access to the tree of life was disinherited. In Revelation access to the tree of life is reinherited. In Genesis we see the beginning of sorrow and death. In Revelation we see the end of sorrow and death. In Genesis man's dominion is broken. In Revelation we see man's dominion restored. In Genesis we see the evil triumph of Satan. In Revelation we see the ultimate triumph of the Lamb. In Revelation, God's walk with man was interrupted. In Revelation, God's walk with man resumes. In Genesis we see Paradise lost. In Revelation we see Paradise regained.

Genesis is the foundation stone; Revelation is the capstone.

WE WILL BEHOLD HIM!

Don't miss the main point of this scene. John saw the glorified Christ—actually, visually, personally. Face to face. Eye to eye. There is coming a day when, as believers, you and I will be ushered into the very presence of Jesus Christ.

167

In that precious moment, we, too, will behold Him through glorified eyes. Then faith will give way to sight. We will see Him—slain, standing, sovereign, searching—just as John saw Him. Our hearts will be overwhelmed with this incredible sight.

I will never forget hearing the story of William Monteague Dyke. Stricken with blindness at the tender age of ten, his life and world were severely limited at an age when other boys were expanding their horizons.

Despite this handicap, this remarkable young man distinguished himself from his peers in more ways than one. William was a very intelligent, witty, and handsome young man who excelled in the classroom. Because of his academic achievements, he won a scholarship to a prestigious graduate school in England.

As if scripted by Hollywood, there William met the beautiful daughter of a British admiral. A courtship soon kindled and flamed into a romance. Though having never seen her, William fell in love with the beauty of her soul. The two became engaged.

Shortly before the wedding, at the insistence of the Admiral, William agreed to submit to newly discovered eye surgery for his blindness. With no assurance that the surgery would restore his sight, the doctors delicately cut optic tissue and bandaged William's eyes. He was then confined to bed with his eyes tightly covered until the time of the wedding.

Hoping against hope that the surgery would be a success, William wanted the first sight to be his bride's face coming down the aisle in her flowing, white wedding dress. After years of torturing darkness, William requested that the gauze be removed from his eyes *during* the wedding ceremony—just when his bride made her way down the center aisle.

As the wedding ceremony began, William was escorted out to the front of the church by his father, who served as his best man. William's eyes and head were still fully bandaged. The dramatic moment was now here, and every eye in the church was upon William.

The organ signaled for his bride to come down the aisle. The back doors of the church swung open and she proceeded in, escorted on the arm of her Admiral father. Every heart waited with anxious anticipation to see what would happen. As his bride came down the center aisle, William's father began carefully unwrapping the long strips of gauze from around his head and eyes—still not knowing if the operation would be a success.

As his wife-to-be stood at the front of the church—in all her glory—the last circumference of the bandage was unwrapped.

And William's eyelids opened.

Light flooded into his heart.

Slowly, William focused ahead, and then looked intently into the radiant face of his precious bride—for the very first time. He could see!

Tears burst from his now healed eyes.

He beheld her beauty!

Overcome with emotion, William whispered, "You are more beautiful than I ever imagined."

Let me assure you, we will experience a scene much like that one day in Heaven. Like the young bridegroom, we, the Church, have never yet seen Jesus Christ our Lord. Peter writes, "Though you have not seen Him, you love Him, and though you do not see Him now, but believe in Him, you greatly rejoice with joy inexpressible and full of glory" (1 Peter 1:8).

In that day, we will be presented to Christ as His bride. We will behold Him face to face! And we will say in absolute wonder, "My Lord, You are more holy and loving than I ever imagined."

Scripture assures us that "we shall see Him just as He is" (1 John 3:2). What a sight! We will see Jesus Christ in all His sovereign glory.

Like William Monteague Dyke, our blinded eyes will be opened, and for the very first time we will see Jesus Christ in all His sovereign splendor. We will see His nail-pierced hands and feet. We will gaze upon His wounded side. Then we will understand more fully the great price He paid upon the cross for us. And we will surely say to Him, "Lord, Jesus, You're more beautiful than I ever imagined You to be."

On that day, Heaven's throne room will be packed with redeemed saints from all the ages. The anticipation will be unequaled. In that moment, the sun will be extinguished. And Jesus Christ will walk out onto the center stage of all the universe. Then believers, young and old, will behold Him in all His glory. Forever. And ever.

Ne plus uttra!
There is nothing beyond!

NOTES
1. William Hendrickson, *More Than Conquerors* (Grand Rapids, MI: Baker, 1991), page 206.
2. R. C. Sproul, *Surprised by Suffering* (Wheaton, IL: Tyndale, 1989), page 171.
3. John MacArthur, *Heaven* (Panorama City, CA: Word of Grace Publications, 1988), page 90.

Chapter Ten

BOTTOM LINE...
ARE YOU READY?

The Preparation For Heaven

Revelation 22:6-21

⁓

OU KNOW WHAT THE BOTTOM LINE IS, DON'T YOU?
The bottom line is an accounting term taken from the world of finance. Back in my college days, I was a finance major and I learned very quickly the importance of the bottom line. In fact, the bottom line is called the bottom line because that's where it appears on a financial statement—on the bottom line.

After adding up all your assets—your cash, bank balances, CDs, properties, equipment, and possessions—and after subtracting out all your liabilities—your debts, money owed, balance on bank loans, as well as any depreciation—you are left with your net worth, which is totaled on the bottom line.

The bottom line tells you where you stand financially. Whether you have a profit or a loss. Whether you are in the black or in the red. Whether you made money or lost money. Forget the details. Never mind all the minutiae. Bottom line, where do you stand?

That's precisely where we are in our study of Heaven. We've come now to the bottom line. The issue before us is, "Am I ready for Heaven? Am I prepared to go to Heaven? Am I going to Heaven? Where do I stand *spiritually*?"

Our study in this book would be utterly meaningless if, bottom line, we are not ready for Heaven. I want us to look at the closing verses of Revelation and discover five keys to prepare us to live with God forever. Without these five key elements, Heaven will take us by surprise. But with them, we'll be packed and ready to go. Here's what each of us must have if we are to be radically prepared for Heaven.

Bottom line . . . are you ready?

AN EXPECTANT ATTITUDE

Being ready for Heaven requires an expectant attitude that eagerly looks for the second coming of Jesus Christ from Heaven. It involves having an anticipation that eagerly awaits the return of Christ and being taken to Heaven.

> *And He said to me, "These words are faithful and true"; and the Lord, the God of the spirits of the prophets, sent His angel to show to His bond-servants the things which must shortly take place. "And behold, I am coming quickly. Blessed is he who heeds the words of the prophecy of this book."* (Revelation 22:6-7)

We must believe that Jesus Christ can come back from Heaven at any moment—today, right now!—and take us home with Him. His coming is imminent. We must live as if Jesus died yesterday, rose this morning, and is coming back *now*! If not, we won't be ready.

The return of Christ, as these verses tell us, "must shortly take place" (verse 6). That means that the time of Christ's return is already upon us. His coming is here. His appearing is the next event on God's prophetic calendar. This blessed hope has been the urgent expectation of the Church for two thousand years, down to this present hour.

Jesus Himself says, "I am coming quickly" (verse 7). These words of our Lord are in the present tense—not the future tense. Jesus is saying, "I am coming *now!*" Not, "I will be coming *later.*"

If we believe that Jesus Christ is coming back today—quickly, imminently, shortly—it will decisively mark the way we live our lives. How so?

By obeying God's Word.

Jesus said, "Blessed is he who heeds the words of the prophecy of this book" (verse 7). The one who heeds—or *obeys*—the word of God is the one who is ready for Heaven. It's not the one who has spiritual "goose bumps" about Heaven. Nor the one who sheds crocodile tears over the truth of Revelation. Nor the one who shouts the loudest or jumps the highest about the Second Coming. But the one who obeys God's Word, that's the one who is ready for Christ's return.

The book of Revelation was not written to *feed* our fascination about the future, but to cause us to *heed* the commands of God. The apocalypse is not given for drafting intricate eschatalogical charts, but for pointing our lives unto godliness.

The Bible says, "When He appears, we shall be like Him, because we shall see Him just as He is. And everyone who has this hope fixed on Him purifies himself, just as He is pure" (1 John 3:2-3). Readiness for Christ's return produces personal holiness.

I heard about a second-grade class that received word that the principal was coming to inspect their room during the upcoming week. The exact time of his visit, however, was unknown.

One little girl said to her classmate, "Aren't you going to clean up your desk? You know the principal is coming."

Her friend replied, "Oh, I'll pick it up tomorrow."

"But, what if," the other little girl asked, "he comes today?"

"Well, I'll pick it up this afternoon."

"But, what if he comes this morning?"

"Well, I'll pick it up after recess."

"But what if he comes before recess?"

The little girl thought a moment and said, "I think I'd better clean up my desk now—and keep it clean!"

That's the way we need to be regarding the Second Coming of Christ and Heaven. We need to clean up our lives now—and keep them clean.

What areas of your life do you need to clean up? Where is your obedience lacking? What have you put off getting ready for Christ's return?

A WORSHIPFUL SPIRIT

If we are to be ready for Heaven, a spirit of worship must fill our hearts each and every day. Heaven must inflame our worship of Christ today.

> *And I, John, am the one who heard and saw these things. And when I heard and saw, I fell down to worship at the feet of the angel who showed me these things. And he said to me, "Do not do that; I am a fellow servant of yours and of your brethren the prophets and of those who heed the words of this book; worship God."*
> (Revelation 22:8-9)

After John heard this message from the angel, he responded with worship—as must we—but his worship was misdirected. Right activity, wrong direction.

John testifies that he has personally seen and heard all of the glorious visions and voices of Heaven recorded in Revelation. But the apostle is so emotionally overwhelmed that he trembles and collapses at the feet of the angel who brings this message. The bewildered prophet loses his bearings. He is so overwhelmed by the awesomeness of the glory of Jesus Christ in Heaven that he falls down to worship the angel.

Of course, John knows better. But in the excitement of the moment, he becomes disoriented. Perhaps it was the fact that Christ had just spoken that threw him off (verse 7). Or maybe it was the dazzling appearance of the angel. Whatever, his emotions got the best of him.

The angel says to John, "Get up! Don't worship me! Get back on your feet! I am only a fellow servant of God as you are. I'm only a mouthpiece for God like you are."

Instead, the angel redirects John's worship toward God. The angelic messenger does *not* say, "This is not the time for worship." *Nor* does he say, "Worship is an inappropriate response to the visions of Heaven." Rather, he says, "Keep on worshiping! Just worship God." In other words, "This is an entirely proper activity—just redirect it toward God!"

The word for worship (*proskuneo*) means to kiss toward, to show affection toward, to bow down before a superior,

175

and give him the respect, reverence, awe, and adoration due him. To worship God means to ascribe the greatness due His name from a heart of love that is humbled and bowed low before His throne.

The psalmist invites us, "Worship the LORD with reverence, and rejoice with trembling. Do homage to [kiss] the Son" (Psalm 2:11-12).

This must be our response too. Bottom line, has the study of Heaven caused you to love Jesus Christ more? Has it caused you to worship Him more? Has it caused you to adore Him more?

No other book in all the Bible ought to cause our hearts to worship Christ more than the book of Revelation. No other book unveils the glories of the risen Christ more than Revelation. In fact, that's what the title Revelation means—this book is the unveiling of Christ. Therefore, no other book so breeds the worship of Christ in our hearts as does this book. The worship of Heaven must inspire worship in our hearts now.

A BELIEVING HEART

The study of Heaven, of course, should make us want to go there. And there is only one way to get to Heaven—that's through personal faith in Jesus Christ. John turns from addressing believers (verses 6-9) to unbelievers, issuing one last call to them to believe in our Lord Jesus Christ:

And He said to me, "Do not seal up the words of the prophecy of this book, for the time is near. Let the one who does wrong, still do wrong; and the one who is filthy, still be filthy; and let the one who is righteous, still practice righteousness; and let the one who is holy, still keep himself holy. Behold, I am coming quickly and my reward is with Me, to render to every man according to what he has done. I am the Alpha and the Omega, the first and the last, the beginning and the end." Blessed are those who wash their robes, that they may have the right to the tree of life, and may enter by the gates into the city. Outside are the dogs and the sorcerers and the immoral persons and the murderers and the idolaters, and every-one who loves and practices lying. "I, Jesus, have sent My angel to testify to you these things for the churches. I am the root and the offspring of David, the bright morning star." And the Spirit and the bride say, "Come." And let the one who hears say, "Come." And let the one who is thirsty come; let the one who wishes take the water of life without cost. (Revelation 22:10-17)

The realities of Heaven and eternity call each one of us to exercise personal faith in Jesus Christ. This decision to believe upon Christ must be done now because, "The time is near." The signs of the times tell us that the return of Christ is soon. We are surely living at the end of the age and Christ's coming is upon us. God is riding across the horizon with boxcar letters for all to see—Jesus is coming! The time is near!

The study of Revelation is a fork in the road that forces us to decide which one of two paths we will take. Heaven or hell? We must choose now where we will spend all eternity. Jesus is coming so quickly that when He does appear, men will have no time in that hour to repent and be saved. Do not put off making a decision for Christ. Heaven can be yours now, but you must receive Christ today if you are to be saved.

When Christ returns, all people will be forever fixed in the spiritual state in which God finds them. The one who is unrighteous at His return will continue to be unrighteous throughout all eternity. And the one who is holy at Christ's return will be holy forever after His return. There will be no second chance to change!

Jesus says, "My reward is with Me to render to every man according to what He has done." This is both positive and negative. Christ is coming to settle His accounts. For the one who has "done wrong" and is "filthy," that person will be paid back judgment, damnation, and hell. But for the one who is "righteous" and "holy," that person will be paid back blessing and happiness.

How blessed are those who, through faith in Christ,

wash their robes and have the right to enter into the new Jerusalem and eat from the tree of life. Those who have been washed clean by the blood of Christ will one day enter Heaven.

Conversely, those who have rejected the gospel will be far away from the new Jerusalem. They are the dogs, Jesus said, an Eastern term of contempt for all who are morally vile and unclean. Oriental dogs were scavengers that were looked down upon with great disdain. These are those unbelievers who are impure and defiled by long contact with the filth of this world.

Joining these vile unbelievers, John said, are *the sorcerers*, those who are false worshipers of various kinds, *the immoral persons*, those who are sexually impure and perverted, *murderers*, those who place no value on human life, *idolaters*, those who live for anything or anyone other than God, and *liars*, those who believe the Devil's lies and false religion.

All these will be excluded from Heaven and consigned to the Lake of Fire. They will be forever shut out of Heaven because they closed their hearts toward Christ and refused to receive Him as their Lord and Savior.

We can believe these sobering realities because it is Jesus Christ Himself who testifies to us about these things. Jesus Christ, who is faithful and true, cannot lie about these eternal matters. He who is the root and offspring of David—meaning both the ancestor and descendant of David—and He who is the bright morning star—the One who will burst upon the scene of human history at its darkest hour—is the One who testifies to these truths.

In response to this urgent appeal to believe while there is time, the Holy Spirit and the Church call out with one voice, "Come!" Here is the heartfelt prayer of every Spirit-filled Christian saying, "Come, Lord Jesus, and take us to Heaven! Come now and take us home to glory."

Isn't this the longing of your heart? Doesn't the Holy Spirit within you stir your heart to cry out to Christ to return now?

Sometimes our hearts become too attached to this

world. But the Spirit within our hearts cries out for Christ to return and sever us from our love for this world. "Maranatha" (1 Corinthians 16:22)—Come, Lord Jesus!

There is a longing expectancy in Christ's heart, as well, for unconverted people to come to Himself and be saved. So Christ now calls out to a lost and dying world to come and drink of His grace. Christ invites every lost sinner to take a step of faith and respond to His gracious appeal. Men must come to Christ as a thirsty man would come to water and drink freely. As a thirsty man opens his mouth and guzzles down a cool, refreshing drink of water, so everyone must open his or her heart and receive Christ.

Whoever wishes to come to Christ must do so today. This invitation is extended to every soul that has ever lived. The offer is as wide as the world is wide. It is as broad as the human race is broad.

Jesus said, "Whoever drinks of the water that I shall give him shall never thirst; but the water that I shall give him shall become in him a well of water springing up to eternal life" (John 4:14).

The story is told of a little, emaciated boy from a large, impoverished family, who was taken to a hospital because of starvation and malnutrition. There in the hospital, a kind nurse came to the starving lad with a big glass of cold milk in her hand.

She gave it to the little fellow and said, "Drink!"

With eager hands, the lad took the glass of milk and asked, "Nurse, how deep can I drink?"

What a picture of poverty he was! Every glass of milk the little boy had ever had was divided with his brothers and sisters. Each sibling could drink just so much, just so far down the glass. There was never enough to go around.

The nurse replied, "Dear child, drink to the bottom, drink to the full."

That's what Christ says to us today. "Come to the waters of life and drink to the full." No matter how famished your heart, how starved your soul, this water will satisfy forever.

If you are to go to Heaven, you must put your full faith in Jesus Christ who died upon the cross for your sins. You must repent and turn from your sin to Christ if you are to receive from Him the free gift of eternal life.

A SOBER MIND

While an invitation is given to all who will listen (Revelation 22:17), a word of warning is now given to those who reject its message (22:18-19). We must be careful never to tamper with the message of God's Word. What John has recorded in the book of Revelation is *God's* Word to us, not man's.

> *I testify to everyone who hears the words of the prophecy of this book: If anyone adds to them, God shall add to him the plagues which are written in this book; and if anyone takes away from the words of the book of this prophecy, God shall take away His part from the tree of life and from the holy city, which are written in this book.*
> (Revelation 22:18-19)

Jesus presses upon us both the truthfulness and the seriousness of what has been revealed to John. If anyone attempts to change God's Word about Heaven, God will add to them the plagues that are described in the Great Tribulation (Revelation 6—18). And if anyone tries to spiritualize away these truths about eternity, God will forever deny them access to the eternal blessings of Christ in Heaven.

It is a serious matter to distort, delude, or deny the truth about the Second Coming of Christ and Heaven. This does not mean that a person once saved can or will lose his or her salvation. Rather, this person will show his or her true colors by taking away from this book and provide conclusive evidence that he was already lost.

Here is a word of caution to each and every one of us. The truth we have looked at from Revelation 4–5 and 21–22 is God's unchangeable message. We must believe all the truths contained herein with all our hearts. To attempt to explain any of it away will bring great harm upon our souls. God is serious about what He has said in His Word, and so must we be.

A CONFIDENT HOPE

Finally, we are ready for Heaven to the extent that we have absolute certainty that Christ is returning soon and eternity is ready to break upon us. John concludes the book of Revelation by saying:

> *He who testifies to these things says, "Yes, I am coming quickly." Amen. Come, Lord Jesus. The grace of the Lord Jesus be with all. Amen.* (Revelation 22:20-21)

Jesus testifies for the third time in these closing verses that He is coming immediately. Jesus says, "I am coming quickly." This is in the present tense. Jesus wants us to know that His coming is so soon, He is already on the way. He is ready to burst upon the scene of human history right now.

The word *quickly* (*tachu*) means immediately, rapidly, imminently, swiftly. In other words, His coming is very, very soon. It is here upon us.

The Bible says, "The coming of the Lord is at hand. . . . Behold, the Judge is standing right at the door" (James 5:8-9).

Jesus said, "Be dressed in readiness, and keep your lamps alight. And be like men who are waiting for their master when he returns from the wedding feast, so that they may immediately open the door to him when he comes and knocks" (Luke 12:35-36). The scene is the middle of the night. While others are asleep, you must be awake, alert, and ready. So much so that throughout the night your hand is on the door, ready to open it the split second Christ knocks at His return.

We should always live every moment of every day as if Christ were coming *now*! That's how to be ready for Heaven! Are you ready? Do you need to witness to someone? Do it *now*! Do you need to be reconciled with someone? Do it *now*! Do you need to be faithful in your financial stewardship? Do it *now*!

John testifies that He is ready. He says, "Amen. Come, Lord Jesus." This means that John believes with all of his heart that Heaven is a real place and that Christ is returning to take him there. So John now says to Christ, "Come and take me to Heaven! Come and take me out of this world and bring me into your glorious presence."

The book of Revelation ends with a closing benediction, "The grace of the Lord Jesus be with all." This is a declaration that God's grace will be poured out upon His children while we wait eagerly for the return of Christ. In these last days of human history, those moments immediately preceding the return of Christ, God's grace is sufficient to carry us through every challenge and fiery trial we will face.

Grace succinctly summarizes all the blessings that are ours in Christ. The grace that saves us will, likewise, enables us to stand strong in these last days. The Old Testament ended with a curse, but the New Testament ends with a blessing. To the very end, God's grace is offered to all who will believe.

The last word of the book of Revelation—and the last word of the Bible—is the word *Amen.* Here is the affirmation of John to certify that he believes all that has been revealed to him in this vision. It is as if John is saying, "I believe it, God! Yes! Just do it, God! Surely, this is all true! I believe there is a place called Heaven. And I believe that Jesus is the Savior and the only way to Heaven."

So, there they are—the five keys to prepare yourself for Heaven:

◆*An expectant attitude* (verses 6-7)
◆*A worshipful spirit* (verses 8-9)
◆*A believing heart* (verses 10-17)
◆*A sober mind* (verses 18-19)
◆*A confident hope* (verses 20-21)

Do you see these five qualities evident in your life? Are you prepared for Heaven? Are you ready to go home?

THE DEADLY MYTH DEFUSED

I said at the beginning of this book that I want to destroy a deadly myth. One so subtle that it hardly seems dangerous. But one so lethal it would delude our faith and damage our walk with Christ.

What is that deadly myth?

"He's so heavenly minded, he's no earthly good."

Don't you believe it.

Just the opposite is true. We *must* be heavenly minded if we are to be any earthly good. Heaven must impact our lives today. Every day we must set our minds on things above where Christ is seated at the right hand of God (Colossians 3:2-3).

This book has been an ardent call from the pages of Revelation 4–5 and 21–22, sounded to reorient our thinking and refocus our hearts toward Heaven. Every decision we make must be made in light of eternity. Every investment of our lives must be made from the perspective of Heaven. In the midst of our hectic schedules and fast-paced lifestyles, we must choose to preoccupy ourselves with the unseen world above where Christ is enthroned as Lord over all.

Let us live for the world to come, not for this present age. Let us live for what is *timeless*, not temporal. Let us live for the *spiritual*, not the earthly. Let us live for the *invisible*, not the visible.

There is a restless longing in every person's heart. God has placed eternity within us (Ecclesiastes 3:11)—a strong desire for the world to come. Whether we realize it or not, our souls long for a place called Heaven. This yearning for our home above calls us to live radically different from those of the world.

Only by setting our sights on Heaven can we find our way through the confusing maze of this world. Without fixing our gaze on God's throne above, we are certain to lose our way and self-destruct.

Sailors who navigate the open sea know there is only one sure way to chart their course and set their direction. Under the dark cloak of night, navigators know that there is only one unchanging reference point by which they may establish their way.

That fixed point?

The north star.

In the uncertainty of night, mariners know that the

north star above is the only reliable compass by which they may navigate the open seas.

That's exactly what God calls us to do through our study of Heaven. As we sail the unchartered seas of life under the veil of night, we must establish our direction and set our course by the unchanging heavens above. If we fail to fix our eyes on Heaven, we will become lost, disoriented, and ultimately, shipwreck our souls.

Many lives have been lost in the vast, open sea of this world and have been unexpectedly sunk by unseen, jagged reefs lurking beneath the surface. All because people failed to navigate their lives by the bright lights of Heaven above.

Don't let this happen to you. Set your mind on things above, not on the things of this earth. Establish your direction and set your course by Heaven.

Remember, this deadly myth will destroy you.

"He's so heavenly minded, he's no earthly good."

Don't you believe it!

When We All Get to Heaven

The Mysteries of Heaven

MANY QUESTIONS MAY REMAIN UNANSWERED in our minds about Heaven. What will our bodies look like in Heaven? Will we know each other? What will we do forever? Will we be able to see what's happening on earth? How old will we be? Will we be married?

These questions, and many more, flood our minds as we think about our eternal home. Obviously, we are riddled with more questions than answers because so much of Heaven remains a mystery.

However, there are clear, biblical answers for many of our intriguing questions. So, let's try to answer some of the most asked questions about Heaven.

DO BELIEVERS GO TO HEAVEN IMMEDIATELY AFTER WE DIE?

Absolutely. At the moment of death, the spirit departs the body and goes immediately to Heaven. Paul wrote, "To be absent from the body [is] to be at home with the Lord" (2 Corinthians 5:8).

That's what happened when Jesus died. At the moment of His death upon the cross, Jesus cried out with a loud voice, saying, "Father, into Thy hands I commit My spirit" (Luke 24:46). And then He breathed His last. When Jesus died, He released His human spirit into the presence of God.

Likewise, that's what happened to the dying thief on the cross. When asked to remember him, Jesus assured him, "*Today*, you shall be with Me in Paradise" (Luke 24:43).

The same will be true for all believers in Christ. When we die, our bodies will be placed in the grave, but our spirits will go directly to Heaven into God's presence. There is no purgatory. No limbo. No soul-sleep. No intermediate state.

I heard about a man named Mr. Peas who died and on his tombstone, they wrote:

"This ain't Peas, it's his pod.
Peas shelled out and went to God."

The Bible says, "The Lord Himself will descend from heaven with a shout, with the voice of the archangel, and with the trumpet of God; and the dead in Christ shall rise first. Then, we who are alive and remain shall be caught up together with them in the clouds to meet the Lord in the air" (1 Thessalonians 4:16-17).

Whenever I perform a graveside service, I always say, "As we commit this body to the grave, let us remember that this is really not our brother lying here. The real person is already in Heaven with the Lord. This is just the body."

HOW WILL WE GET TO HEAVEN?
Scripture indicates that when we die an angel will escort our departed spirit to Heaven. That was the case with a poor man named Lazarus: "Now it came about that the poor man died and he was carried by the angels to Abraham's bosom" (Luke 16:22).

Certainly, living saints have been taken to Heaven dramatically in different ways. Elijah was taken up to Heaven in a chariot of fire in a whirlwind (2 Kings 2:11). Enoch was walking one day and simply disappeared (Genesis 5:22-24). Jesus ascended to Heaven in a cloud (Acts 1:9-11). Believers will be personally ushered to Heaven by an angel.

WHAT WILL OUR BODIES BE LIKE IN HEAVEN?
Interestingly enough, we will have glorified bodies that will resemble our Lord's resurrected body exactly. We will not be disembodied spirits without bodily form.

Writing to the Corinthians, the Apostle Paul provides a more detailed preview of what the heavenly bodies of beliveres will be like. Specifically, he writes, "But someone will say, 'How are the dead raised? and with what kind of body do they come?'" (1 Corinthians 15:35). In the follow-

187

ing verses (verses 38-49), the apostle answers this thought-provoking question.

Individual Bodies
When we get to Heaven, we're not all going to be look-alike clones. We will retain our own individual identity. Paul explains, "God gives it a body just as He wished, and to each of the seeds a body of its own" (1 Corinthians 15:38). Just as a seed is placed in the ground and dies, it nevertheless reproduces the same life form. A barley seed produces barley. And a wheat seed produces wheat.

In similar fashion, our bodies will have a recognizable continuity from this life to our heavenly life. Like a seed placed in the ground, our earthly bodies will die and change form, but they will still be our individual bodies.

Imperishable Bodies
Paul continues, "It is sown a perishable body, it is raised an imperishable body" (1 Corinthians 15:42). Our present bodies are perishable and subject to deterioration, disease, death, and decay. From the moment we are born, the aging process begins. With every passing day, we look more and more like a million dollars—all green and wrinkled.

But, one day, we will receive an imperishable body—one that is not subject to the downward spiral of decay. Our heavenly bodies will never experience any sickness, decay, or deterioration because "this mortal will have put on immortality" (15:54).

Glorious Bodies
Paul adds, "It is sown in dishonor; it is raised in glory" (1 Corinthians 15:43). Our present bodies are limited in their ability to glorify God. But, in our new resurrection bodies, we will have the unlimited potential to honor God. We will be able to please Him in unprecedented fashion.

Powerful Bodies
The apostle writes, "It is sown in weakness; it is raised in power" (1 Corinthians 15:43). In these earthly bodies, we

are always subject to loss of energy and physical limitations. We want to serve God more, but we have to sleep. We want to pray and study the Bible, but we grow weary. In Heaven, bodies will do whatever we want them to do. We will possess boundless energy with which to serve God.

Spiritual Bodies

Paul explains, "It is sown a natural body; it is raised a spiritual body. If there is a natural body, there is also a spiritual body" (1 Corinthians 15:44).

A new body, perfectly adapted to the new heavenly environment, will be given to us. We could no more live in Heaven with our earthly body than we could live under the ocean. Likewise, if we were going to live under water, we would need a body adapted to the environment—one with gills, scales, and a fin. In the same way, if we are going to live in Heaven, we need a new body perfectly suited for our new heavenly surroundings.

Christlike Bodies

Our bodies will be powerfully overhauled into perfect conformity with the risen, glorified body of Christ.

> *So also it is written, "The first man, Adam, became a living soul." The last Adam became a life-giving spirit. However, the spiritual is not first, but the natural; then the spiritual. The first man is from the earth, earthy; the second man is from Heaven. As is the earthy, so also are those who are earthy; and as is the heavenly, so also are those who are heavenly. And just as we have borne the image of the earthy, we shall also bear the image of the heavenly.* (1 Corinthians 15:45-49)

Think about Jesus' resurrection body. He could walk through walls (John 20:19), travel through space (Acts 1:9-11), mysteriously appear (Luke 24:31), and suddenly disappear. He was recognized by men (John 20:16), yet sometimes unrecognized (Luke 24:16). He could talk, walk, sit, eat, and drink (1 John 2:4-9). Similarly, we will be clothed with a new body, just like Christ's post-resurrection body, with unusual ability for supernatural travel, speech, and service.

WILL WE KNOW EACH OTHER IN HEAVEN?

Of course! Charles H. Spurgeon once remarked, "We knew one another on earth. Will we be bigger fools in Heaven?"

Dr. W. A. Criswell, beloved pastor of the First Baptist Church of Dallas, was once asked, "Will we know each other when we get to Heaven?"

"We won't really know each other," he replied, "{until} we get to Heaven."

At a college reunion, thirty years after graduation, one man said to another, "See that fellow over there? He's gotten so bald and so fat, he didn't even recognize me!"

Well, in our heavenly reunion, we {will} recognize each other.

In Heaven, we will retain our own personal earthly identity and recognize one another. For example, on the Mount of Transfiguration, Moses and Elijah were immediately recognized by Peter, James, and John.

Jesus promised, "I say to you, that many shall come from east and west and recline at the table with Abraham, Isaac, and Jacob in the kingdom of Heaven" (Matthew 8:11). Obviously, Abraham, Isaac, and Jacob will be there in Heaven, maintaining their same identity—and we will know them.

We will recognize the saints of all the ages, including our loved ones. We will have fellowship with Old Testament heroes of the faith—men and women like Noah, Abraham, Moses, Joshua, Ruth, Elijah, Isaiah, David, Esther—and with New Testament believers like Peter, Paul, and John, as well as mighty men and women from church history, like John Calvin, John Wesley, and so on.

HOW OLD WILL WE BE?

Scripture doesn't tell us, so any answer is pure conjecture. Some have suggested age thirty-three since Christ was thirty-three, or thereabouts, when He was crucified.

That's certainly possible. After all, we will be made like Christ's resurrection body (Philippians 3:20), and Jesus was in His early thirties when He was raised from the dead.

But, remember this—in eternity, there is no time, consequently, there is no age. Age implies aging, and we will never age in Heaven. So, perhaps there is no age in Heaven.

WILL WE EAT AND DRINK IN HEAVEN?

Yes, we will eat and drink in Heaven as Jesus ate and drank in His resurrection body. On one occasion when Jesus appeared to His disciples after His resurrection, He ate with them. "They gave Him a piece of a broiled fish, and He took it and ate it before them" (Luke 24:43).

Likewise, Jesus instituted the Lord's Supper and said, "For I say to you, I will not drink of the fruit of the vine from now on until the kingdom of God comes" (Luke 22:18). So, He promises to eat and drink with us after the Second Coming, just as He participated with His disciples at the first Lord's Supper.

At the time of the Second Coming, saints in Heaven will enjoy "the marriage supper of the Lamb" (Revelation 19:9). Such a supper clearly implies eating with Christ, the Bridegroom. In the new Jerusalem, we will eat the fruit and leaves of the tree of life (Revelation 22:3). And, in Heaven, we will gather around a banquet table with the patriarchs and surely eat (Matthew 8:11).

Why will we eat and drink in Heaven? For the sheer pleasure of it, not out of any need for physical sustenance. Our glorified bodies will be endowed with supernatural power that will never diminish. We will eat to our heart's delight, and never gain weight!

WILL WE BE MARRIED IN HEAVEN?

No, no one in Heaven will be married. The institution of marriage is a part of this world order, which is passing away. Because "the form of this world is passing away," so will marriage with it (1 Corinthians 7:31).

During the days of His earthly ministry, some Sadducees

tried to trap Christ with a question about marriage in Heaven.

> *"Teacher, Moses said, 'If a man dies, having no children, his brother as next of kin shall marry his wife and raise up an offspring to his brother.' Now, there were seven brothers with us: and the first married and died, and having no offspring left his wife to his brother; so also the second and the third, down the to the seventh. And last of all, the woman died. In the resurrection, therefore, whose wife of the seven shall she be? For they all had her."* (Matthew 22:24-28)

The amazing thing about this question is that these liberal Sadducees didn't even believe in the resurrection. They were simply attempting to discredit Jesus publicly.

Jesus answered, "For in the resurrection they neither marry, nor are given in marriage, but are like angels in heaven" (verse 30). In other words, marriage lasts only for this life. We will not be married in Heaven because it will be unnecessary. Men won't need a helper, and women won't need a protector. Certainly, the need for procreation will have passed away.

Now, before you get too sad about this (although some of you are shouting "Amen!"), let me tell you that, although unmarried, you will be exponentially closer to your spouse in Heaven than the happiest day of your marriage here. Your relationship will be far more meaningful there because there will be no misunderstandings. No hurt feelings. No selfishness. No impatience. Just perfect love.

Ladies, your husbands will finally communicate and sympathize with you in Heaven!

WILL WE GRIEVE FOR UNSAVED LOVED ONES?
Many of us wonder how we can be happy if an unsaved parent, child, or sibling does not arrive in Heaven. Will we grieve their loss in Heaven? How can we rejoice eternally without them?

These unsaved loved ones will not be remembered in

Heaven. God shall wipe their remembrance from our minds.

The psalmist David writes concerning God's enemies, "The enemy has come to an end in perpetual ruins . . . the very memory of them has perished" (Psalm 9:6). In like manner, God will eternally remove the memory of all His enemies in our minds. All who do not know Christ are ultimately His enemies and will one day be forgotten even by God's people.

DO BABIES WHO DIE GO TO HEAVEN?

I believe babies go to Heaven. Although the Bible does not address the question at great length, the weight of Scripture indicates that little babies and young children do go to Heaven.

When David's baby was deathly sick, he fasted and prayed with a broken heart. Then, tragically, the child died. When David was told the news of his baby's death, he responded, "But now he has died; why should I fast? Can I bring him back again? I shall go to him, but he will not return to me" (2 Samuel 12:23).

David understood that he would be reunited with his child. But the child would not come to him. Rather, David would go to the child, meaning be reunited in Heaven.

Jesus indicates the same: "Let the children alone and do not hinder them from coming to Me; for the kingdom of heaven belongs to such as these" (Matthew 19:14).

Also, the praise of Heaven says, "Thou was slain and didst purchase for God with Thy blood men from every tribe and tongue and people and nation" (Revelation 5:10). The gospel has not been preached to every people group, yet here are representatives from every group on the globe. How is this possible? It can be argued through those who die in infancy before an age of accountability.

WILL WE RELATE TO ANGELS?

Yes, we will have contact with angels in Heaven. First, we will worship closely with them around God's throne. Revelation 4 and 5 make it clear that angels and saints alike will worship together in the same throng. Second, we will fellowship with the angels. Angels and people have communed at various times here on the earth. So, we will rejoice together in Heaven about the greatness of God. Angels rejoice in the triumphs of the gospel (Luke 15:7,10; 1 Peter 1:12), and will join with God's people in exulting in the grace of God.

WHAT WILL WE DO IN HEAVEN?

There will be plenty to do. Don't ever think of Heaven as a boring place. We will be busier than ever before. There will be so much to do, it will take us all eternity to do it. That's one reason God will give us a glorified body—simply to keep up the fast pace of Heaven.

Actually, we will do many of the same things in Heaven that we did here on the earth—just perfectly.

First, we will *worship God*. This will be our primary activity in Heaven. With a pure heart, our worship will be pure, sincere, fervent, and without distraction. In Heaven, we will have a fuller knowledge of God and what He has done than we have now. Consequently, unending praise will burst from our mouths forever.

Second, we will *reign with Christ*. We shall receive administrative responsibility to manage and oversee assignments in Heaven (Revelation 22:5). Each of us will have a specially designed sphere where we will co-reign with Christ over a new created order. The more faithful we are in this life, the more delegated responsibility we will be given in Heaven (Matthew 25:14-21). We will oversee cities (Luke 19:17-19), judge angels (1 Corinthians 6:30), and govern nations (Matthew 19:28).

Third, we will *serve Christ*. In Heaven, we will serve God forever as a kingdom of priests (Revelation 1:6). We will have ministry assignments to carry out in Heaven and derive great satisfaction from serving Him (22:3). We will serve God without time demands, without fear of failure, without physical limitations, and without unnecessary interruptions. We will have all eternity to see, know, enjoy, and get acquainted with each other.

Fourth, we will *fellowship with one another*. In Heaven, we will enjoy limitless opportunities for fellowship, free from all the misunderstandings and petty differences that now divide us. We will relax around the table together (Matthew 8:11) and spend time with loved ones (1 Thessalonians 4:17). There, we will have eternity to get to know and enjoy each other.

Fifth, we will *travel extensively*. In our glorified bodies, we will fly through space to vast new frontiers of the new heavens. We will go in and out of the new Jerusalem and experience the joy of discovering new frontiers of the new creation.

Sixth, we will *rest eternally*. In Heaven, we will rest from our wearisome labors (Revelation 14:13) and exhausting trials (6:11). All our striving against sin and resisting Satan will be over. No longer will a sinful world drain us. At last, we will fully enter into the eternal rest prepared for us by God. Yet, this rest will not be a rest from meaningful work and challenging activity. For the first time, we will be fully rested in serving God.

THE HAPPIEST DAY OF OUR LIVES

Despite all our questions about Heaven, some of them yet unanswered, one truth remains sure. Regardless of what mysteries remain, we can be assured that when we enter into God's presence, it will be the happiest day of our lives. What joy will be ours—ten thousand times ten thousand—just to be in His presence. The psalmist agrees, "In Thy presence is fullness of joy; in Thy right hand there are pleasures forever" (Psalm 16:11).

The day we enter Heaven will be the happiest day of our lives.

Dr. Robert G. Lee, the former pastor of Bellevue Baptist Church in Memphis, Tennessee, told this story from his childhood.[1] One day he found himself at home on the farm with his mother. She was rocking on the front porch, knitting, as young Robert sat at her feet. He cupped his chin in his hands, stuck his heels up in the air, and looked up at his mama.

195

"Mama," he asked, "what was the happiest day in your life?"

His mother rocked and thought awhile. Would she answer the day when his father proposed to her out by the gate on a moonlit night? Or, would it be the time when they stood in the corner of their farmhouse and were married? But that wasn't what she said.

"Son, there was a horrible war between the states, the North against the South, brother against brother. Your granddaddy—my daddy—went to war. There were no men around. My mother worked alongside the other women in the field. We didn't have the things we have today. The only salt we had was what we could scrape off the smokehouse floor. The only coffee we had was dried ground corn. It was a hard time.

"The news came that my daddy had been killed in the war. I cannot tell you how dark that day was. When they told my mother, she wept. We didn't see her weep openly very much during the day, but all night long, I could hear her sobbing—all night long. We did the best we could to get along without daddy, but it was tough to be so alone.

"Then, one day we were sitting on the porch, and my mother looked down the old river road. And she said to me, 'Elizabeth, that man walking down the road so far away . . . he looks like your daddy.' She was snapping beans as she stared across the horizon.

"After a while, as the figure got closer, she said, 'I declare! That man sure does remind me of your daddy.'

"I said to her, 'Now, mama, you know Daddy's dead. Don't get thoughts like that in your head and in your heart.'

"But then that man turned and cut across the cotton patch and started toward our house. My mother suddenly threw the beans in the air, gathered up her skirt, and began to run!

"She flew across the front yard as fast as she could. She'd recognized that the man was my daddy! He had one arm missing—a sleeve pinned up. He embraced my mother with the other arm. They wept and they laughed and they danced.

"I ran as fast as my legs would let me. When I got to them, I put my arms around my daddy's knees and I hugged him and rejoiced that my daddy was home.

"Son, I do believe that was the happiest day of my life."

But, happy as that day was, it will pale into insignificance one day when compared with the glorious moment when we will enter Heaven and come face to face with our Lord Jesus Christ. What joy will be ours!

We have loved Him, though never seen Him. Separated these many years, we long to see Him who died for us.

But, one day, we will be united with Him forever in Heaven. We will see His nail-pierced hands, stretched out with open arms to receive us. We will run before Him as He says, "Welcome home, My child. Enter into the joy that I have prepared for you."

That will be the happiest day of our lives.

Heaven *can't* wait!

NOTE

1. Adapted from Robert G. Lee, quoted by Adrian Rogers, unpublished manuscript on Luke 19:11-24.

AUTHOR

Dr. Steven J. Lawson is the Senior Pastor of Dauphin Way Baptist Church of Mobile, Alabama. He has a B.B.A. from Texas Tech University, a Th.M. from Dallas Theological Seminary, and a D.Min. from Reformed Theological Seminary. A former sportswriter for the Texas Rangers and the Dallas Cowboys, he is also a featured speaker for the Billy Graham Evangelistic Association. Steve is the author of *When All Hell Breaks Loose* and *Men Who Win: Pursuing the Ultimate Prize*, published by NavPress.

Steve and his wife, Anne, have four children.